# EXPLORES ... THE AZTECS

JOHN MALAM

EVANS BROTHERS LIMITED

Evans Brothers Limited
2A Portman Mansions
Chiltern Street
London W1M 1LE



First published 1994

Printed in Spain by GRAFO, S.A. – Bilbao

ISBN 0 237 51219 X

British Library Cataloguing in Publication Data.
A catalogue record for this book is available from the British Library.

## Acknowledgements

The author and publishers would like to thank the following people for their valuable help and advice:

Dr Anne Millard BA (Hons) Dip. ed., Dip. Arc., Ph.D. author, archaeologist and lecturer

Illustrations: Virginia Gray
Maps: Jillie Luff, Bitmap Graphics

Editor: Jean Coppendale
Design: Neil Sayer
Production: Jenny Mulvanny

For permission to reproduce copyright material the author and publishers gratefully acknowledge the following:

Cover photograph: Temples at Chichen Itza, e.t. archive

**Title page:** ceremonial mask inlaid with a mosaic of turquoise and shell, British Museum
**page 8** ZEFA **page 9** ZEFA **page 10** (top) Anthropology Museum, Veracruz University, Jalapa, Werner Forman Archive, (bottom) Dr John B Free, Heritage and Natural History Photography **page 11** (middle left) ZEFA, (middle right) University of Essex, Trip, (bottom) Dr John B Free, Heritage and Natural History Photography **page 12** AKG/Image Select **page 13** The Bodleian Library **page 14** Werner Forman Archive **page 16** (top) Tony Morrison, South American Pictures, (bottom) The Bodleain Library **page 18** (top) CM Dixon, (bottom) The Bodleain Library **page 19** The Bodleian Library **page 20** (top) Museum fur Volkerkunde, (bottom) AKG/Image Select **page 21** e.t. archive **page 22** The Bodleian Library **page 23** National Museum of Anthropology, Mexico City, Werner Forman Archive **page 24** (middle) Dr John B Free, Heritage and Natural History Photography, (bottom) The Bodleian Library **page 25** British Museum **page 26** (left) Ted Stephan, Cephas Picture Library, (right) Dr John B Free, Heritage and Natural History Photography **page 27** (top) The Bodleain Library, (bottom) CM Dixon **page 28** (top) AKG/Image Select, (bottom) Ancient Art and Architecture Collection **page 29** (top left) British Museum, Werner Forman Archive, (middle) British Museum, The Bridgeman Art Library, (bottom) Ancient Art and Architecture Collection **page 31** (top) Liverpool Museum, Werner Forman Archive, (bottom) British Museum, The Bridgeman Art Library **page 32** (left) Wurttembergisches Landesmuseum Stuttgart, Robert Harding Picture Library, (right) University of Essex, Trip **page 33** (top) British Museum, (bottom) British Museum, Werner Forman Archive **page 34** (top) British Museum, Werner Forman Archive, (bottom) British Museum, Werner Forman Archive **page 35** (top left) Robert Frerck, Robert Harding Picture Library, (top right) Dr John B Free, Heritage and Natural History Photography, (bottom) e.t. archive **page 36** (left) ZEFA, (right) CM Dixon **page 40** (left) British Museum, Werner Forman Archive, (right) The Hutchison Library **page 41** (top left) British Museum, (top right) Nick Saunders, Barbara Heller Photo Library, (bottom) e.t. archive **page 42** Giraudon, The Bridgeman Art Library **page 43** (top) Biblioteca Nacional, Madrid, The Bridgeman Art Library, (bottom left)Ancient Art and Architecture Collection, (bottom right) Bilbioteca Nacional, Madrid, The Bridgeman Art Library **page 44** (top) ZEFA, (bottom) Robert Frerck, Robert Harding Picture Library **page 45** (left) CC Lockwood, Bruce Coleman Ltd, (right) Dr John B Free, Heritage and Natural History Photography

# Contents

# TIMELINE OF THE AZTECS

## and the rest of the world

| WORLD HISTORY | | AZTEC HISTORY | |
|---|---|---|---|
| 1200 | Rise of the Inca Empire in Peru | 1200 | The nomadic Aztec tribe reached the Valley of Mexico claiming to be descendants of the warlike Toltecs |
| 1200s | Rise of the Mongol Empire in Asia and Europe | | |
| | | 1200 to 1300 | The Aztecs moved up and down the Valley of Mexico in search of their own land |
| 1271–95 | Marco Polo travelled to China | | |
| 1300s | Great Zimbabwe city built in Africa | 1325 | The traditional date when the Aztecs are said to have settled on an island in Lake Texcoco |
| 1347–53 | Black Death plague in Europe | | |
| | | 1350 to 1400 | The Aztecs built their island capital of Tenochtitlan and conquered tribes throughout the Valley of Mexico |
| 1492 | Christopher Columbus sailed to the 'New World' (America) | 1400 to 1500 | The Aztecs became the strongest tribe in the Valley of Mexico |
| 1510 | The first slaves from Africa were taken to America | 1502 to 1520 | Reign of Moctezuma II, the last great Aztec Emperor |
| | | August 1519 | A small Spanish army, led by Hernán Cortés, arrived in Mexico |
| | | November 1519 | Cortés met Moctezuma at Tenochtitlan. The Aztecs treated the Spaniards as gods. The Spaniards took Moctezuma prisoner |
| 1520 | Magellan sailed across the Pacific Ocean | May to July 1520 | An Aztec uprising almost defeated the Spaniards. Moctezuma was killed in the fighting |
| 1520s | The potato was introduced to Europe from South America | | |
| 1532 | Spaniards made contact with the Incas of Peru, led by Francisco Pizarro. Their empire was looted and destroyed | 1521 | Cortés returned to Tenochtitlan with a large army of Indians opposed to the Aztecs. Disease had killed many of the Aztecs in the city, and after a great battle the Aztecs were defeated. Tenochtitlan was destroyed and the Aztec Empire broke up |
| | | 1547 | Cortés died in Spain |
| 1550s | Tobacco was introduced to Europe from South America | 1567 | Cortés's body was returned to Mexico and buried in the cathedral built from the stones of the Aztecs' Great Temple |
| 1588 | The Spanish Armada was defeated by an English fleet | | |
| | | 1970s | Remains of the Aztecs' Great Temple uncovered by archaeologists |

# Mexico at the time of the Aztecs

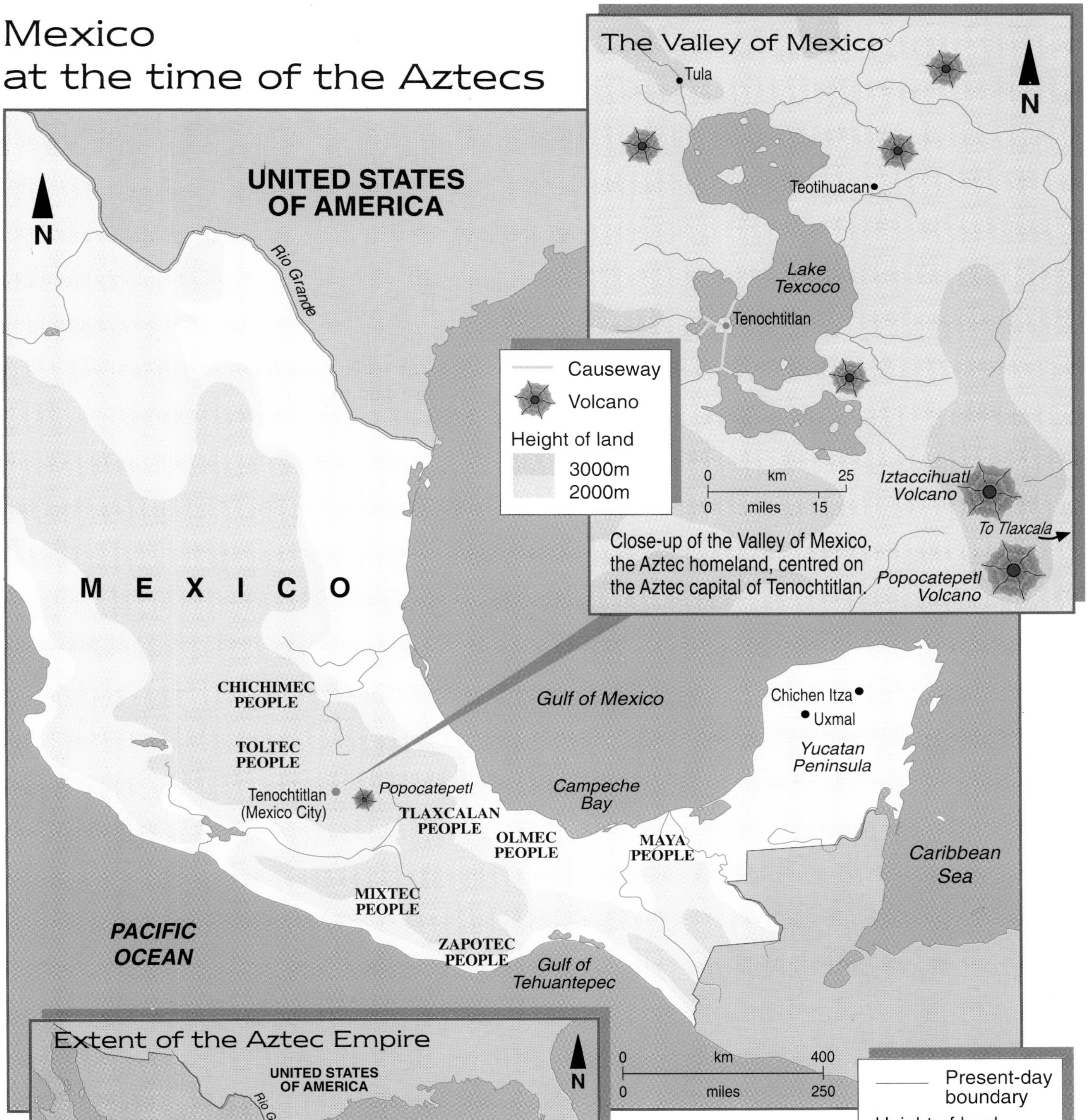

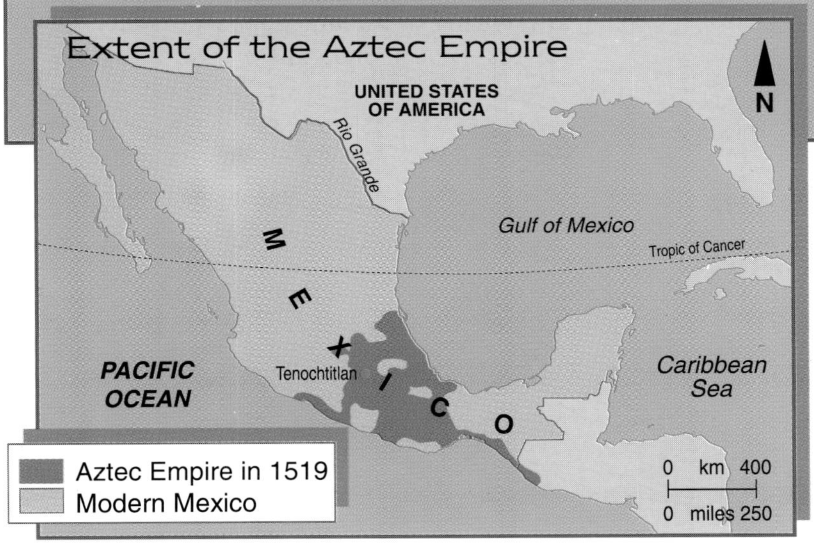

## The Valley of Mexico



Close-up of the Valley of Mexico, the Aztec homeland, centred on the Aztec capital of Tenochtitlan.

## Extent of the Aztec Empire



Left: This map shows the area controlled by the Aztecs at the time of the Spanish conquest in 1519.

# WHO WERE THE AZTECS?

## Introduction to the Aztecs

The day the letter from Mexico City arrived is one I won't forget in a hurry. Professor Miguel Paz of the city's university, and one of Mexico's leading archaeologists, had written to invite me to visit his excavations. He'd found some amazing Aztec remains and, from the photographs he sent with the letter, this looked like an opportunity not to be missed. He'd also enclosed the flight tickets – his way of making sure I wouldn't refuse!

But what did I know about the Aztecs? Before my trip to Mexico I knew little about them – but that changed after I'd spent some time with Professor Paz. He introduced me to the world of the Aztecs – and this is what I want you to explore with me.

During the flight to Mexico City, I decided to read some travel guides. I learned that Mexico is a land of ruined cities, towns and ancient buildings. These are all that remain of once powerful civilizations that developed there – peoples such as the Olmecs, Toltecs, Maya and, of course, the Aztecs.

Popocatepetl, whose name means the Smoking Mountain, is an active volcano that dominates the Valley of Mexico. At 5,456 metres high it is the second highest mountain in Mexico. Spanish soldiers who invaded the Aztec kingdom in the 1500s made gunpowder with sulphur collected from Popocatepetl's smoking crater.

Hernán Cortés, the leader of an invading Spanish army in the 1500s (see page 42), destroyed the Aztec capital of Tenochtitlan. He proclaimed that, "the new city of Mexico shall be built upon the ashes of Tenochtitlan, and as it was the principal and ruling city of all these provinces, so shall it be from this time forward." His wishes have come true, and today Mexico City is a vast, sprawling centre of over fifteen million people. By the year 2000 it could be the most populated city in the world.

Mexico (or the area we now refer to as Mexico) had been occupied by many different groups of people for thousands of years before the arrival of the Aztecs. Each group had its own identity and to the trained eye of an archaeologist the differences between them are clear to see. Two facts struck me as I read the guidebooks. The first was how recently the Aztecs had lived.

Compared with the Ancient Egyptians who lived 5,000 years ago and the Ancient Greeks of 2,500 years ago, the Aztecs were really modern by our standards of time. They flourished only 600 years ago, or to put it another way, about 20 generations of people ago! The second fact to surprise me was that the Aztec civilization lasted for only about 200 years. It might have lasted longer had it not been for the arrival of Europeans in the early 1500s. But their coming brought the Aztec world to a speedy end.

My plane landed at Mexico City's International Airport and soon Professor Paz and I were on our way to Mexico City itself – one of the busiest cities in the world.

Fact File

### Mexico – land of the Aztecs

*Mexico is a large country in Central America. It has one of the most varied landscapes I've ever seen, with deserts, jungles, plains and mountains. There are over 10,000 kilometres of coastline and offshore are coral reefs – but I won't have time to explore them on this trip. As we drove towards Mexico City, Professor Paz told me about the Valley of Mexico – the homeland of several ancient civilizations. He explained that the Valley is at high altitude (about 2,100 metres above sea level) and is about 120 kilometres long and 65 kilometres wide. The Valley is surrounded by mountains and at one end are the snow-capped volcanoes of Popocatepetl ('Smoking Mountain') and Itaccihuatl ('White Lady'). The Valley of Mexico became the centre of the Aztec world, and Tenochtitlan, their capital, became the site of Mexico City, the modern capital. The Aztecs called their land 'Anahuac' which meant the 'land on the edge of the waters'.*

# Mexico before the Aztecs

Professor Paz was keen for me to learn about the people who lived in Mexico before the Aztecs. He said it was important to realize the Aztecs had been only one of many peoples in Mexico and their civilization was based on older ones developed by earlier societies.

In Mexico City we went to the National Museum of Anthropology, a massive place with exhibits of Mexico's wonders from the past. It was too big to see everything on one visit as there are over five kilometres of rooms to walk through! I bought a guidebook to remind me of the things I'd seen. Here is what it said about Mexico before the Aztecs.

**Olmecs (1200 to 400 BC)**
The Olmecs were the first civilization of Mexico. Their influence over later civilizations was so strong that they have been called Mexico's 'mother culture'. They seem to have been warlike because they made carvings of heavily armed warriors. They traded for rare stones such as obsidian and jade from which they carved figures of gods and animals such as the jaguar.

A massive stone head carved by the Olmecs. It is nearly 3 metres high and may represent one of their rulers, but his name is not known. Note how his ear-lobe is pierced and stretched. The wearing of ear ornaments was widely practised amongst the peoples of ancient Central and South America. A total of 16 giant heads carved by the Olmecs have so far been discovered. Traces of paint show that they were brightly decorated.

**Teotihuacan (100 BC to AD 750)**
This was the first great city in Mexico – but we do not know which people lived there. The Aztecs called it the 'city of the gods'. Teotihuacan may have had 200,000 inhabitants, making it larger than ancient Rome. Its streets were built to a grid-pattern and were lined with temple pyramids.

Teotihuacan, the city built by a mysterious and unknown people. At its centre were the great step-pyramids of the sun and moon gods. To give you an idea of how big this pyramid is, look for the people standing at the top of it.

**Toltecs (AD 900 to 1150)**
Toltecs, whose name means 'artists', were the last of the great civilizations before the Aztecs. They were a military people who took over styles of art and building from the people they conquered. From Tula, their capital, they governed their empire by force.

**Maya (300 BC to AD 1500)**
The civilization of the Maya overlapped with that of the Aztecs. The Maya were a sophisticated people who built grand cities. They used a system of picture writing that has only recently been understood.

These stone columns, which are 4 metres high, are at the Toltec capital of Tula. They once held up the roof of a temple dedicated to Quetzalcoatl, the Wind God. This god was worshipped by other people (including the Aztecs), not just the Toltecs. The columns have been carved to look like Toltec.

### Aztecs enter the Valley of Mexico

*In my hotel room that night I turned the pages of the museum guidebook to discover where the Aztecs had come from. I read that they had first entered the Valley of Mexico in about 1200, arriving as a tribe of nomads from a mysterious place in the north of the country called Aztlan, from where the name Aztec comes. At this time the Valley was already heavily populated and there was little land left for the Aztecs. An Aztec story had said their tribe would eventually settle at a place where an eagle on a cactus plant would be seen. In about 1325 this sign appeared on a swampy island in Lake Texcoco. The Aztecs settled on the island and began to build their city of Tenochtitlan, whose name means 'place of the prickly pear cactus'* *(also see page 14)**.*

An Aztec drawing showing the migration route taken by the Aztecs. Aztlan, their island homeland, is shown on the left. After crossing a lake by canoe, footprints mark the way to a cave in a mountain, where a god gave directions which told the tribe to continue travelling south towards the Valley of Mexico.

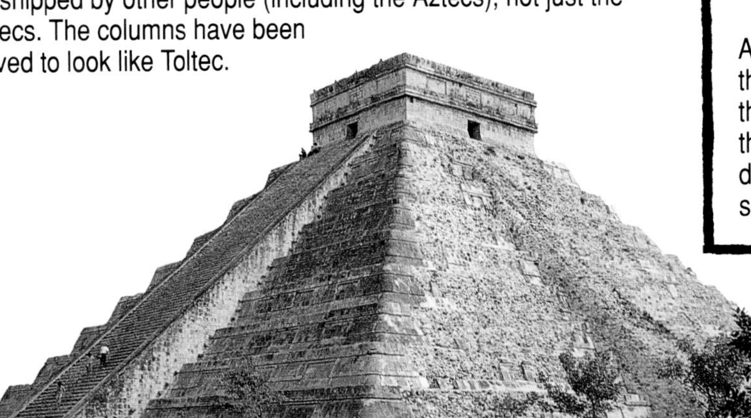

The Maya were skilled at cutting and shaping stone for building. This temple is at the Maya city of Chichen Itza, in the far east of Mexico.

# THE EMPIRE OF THE AZTECS

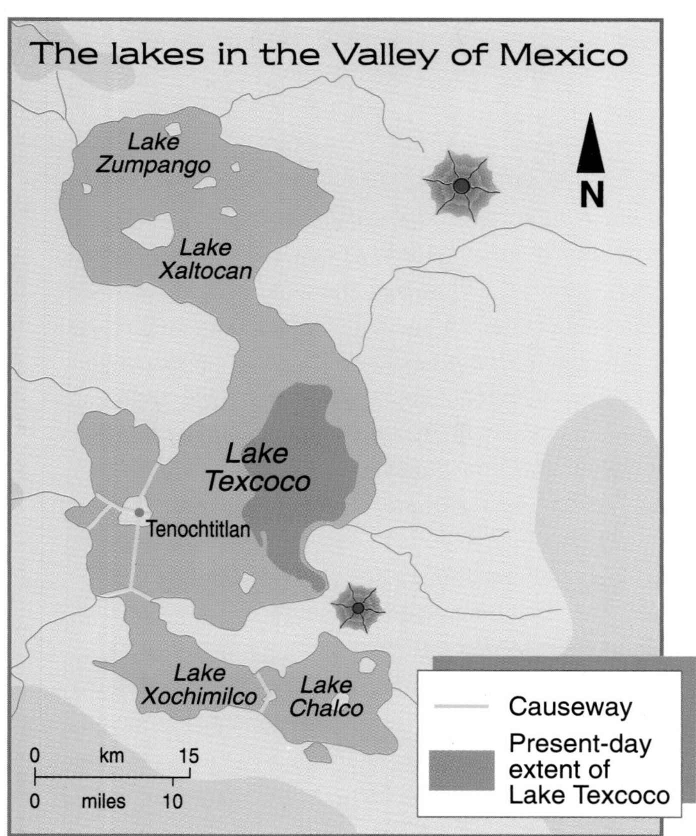


At the time the Aztecs settled on their island in Lake Texcoco there were five connected lakes in the Valley of Mexico. Today, the lakes have nearly disappeared as Mexico City has expanded and drained their shallow waters.

## Starting the empire

People in Mexico and other hot countries usually start work early and finish late at night. During the hottest part of the day they have a three or four hour rest called a 'siesta'. Professor Paz had arranged to show me Mexico City and at just after seven o'clock in the morning I met him at his excavation site – the one he had sent me photographs of.

"Imagine you were standing here 500 years ago," he said. "You would have been on a marshy island surrounded by the waters of Lake Texcoco." Standing in the modern city I found this hard to picture. But then I looked down into the large trench dug by the Professor's workmen and I saw the ghostly shape of an ancient building from another time – a piece of the Aztec city of Tenochtitlan.

But how, I wondered, had the Aztecs become the strongest people in the Valley of Mexico if they lived on an island in a lake? The Professor said that the Aztecs had been newcomers to the Valley and at first they had no land of their own. For about 100 years they wandered up and down the Valley working for people who were already living there. Eventually, the Aztecs were allowed to live on the island because it was of no use to anyone else: it had poor, wet soil and little timber. Despite this, the Aztecs settled there.

Professor Paz conjured up images of the early Aztecs as an unpopular tribe struggling to survive. But far from being a poor place to live, the island had good points which the Aztecs used to their advantage.

The Aztecs took ideas from other tribes, especially the Toltecs from whom they said they were descended. This stone figure is called a 'chacmool'. In its hands is a dish which was used to hold blood and other offerings to the gods. Figures such as this were first made by the Toltecs and copied later by the Aztecs.

Because it was an island it was hard to attack but easy to defend. It was near to the kingdoms of other groups in the Valley and it became a jumping off point for making conquests. The island became a safe place to live.

The Aztecs grew in strength and formed a partnership with other tribes. Between them they ruled the Valley of Mexico and far beyond. When the Aztecs became the strongest tribe they claimed the land as theirs and ruled the other tribes. From the regions they conquered they obtained timber and food. The conquered tribes supplied them with jade, gold, rubber and slaves. The Aztecs became wealthy and could afford to turn Tenochtitlan into a fabulous city.

### Kidnapping history

*History can be used in many different ways. In the wrong hands history can be used like a weapon, turning people against others because the history-teller does not tell the truth. It seems that the Aztecs realized how important history could be for them and that they could turn it to their advantage. When they became the dominant people in the Valley of Mexico they began to claim they were descended from the Toltecs (see page 11). They robbed the Toltec capital of Tula and stripped it of whatever they wanted for their own capital of Tenochtitlan, 75 kilometres to the south. We know the Aztecs were not really connected with the mighty Toltecs – but imagine how powerful it must have made the Aztecs seem when they began spreading this story amongst the tribes around them.*

The Aztecs believed an eagle in a cactus bush was the sign that would show them where they would eventually settle. The sign appeared in about 1325, the traditional date for the founding of their capital Tenochtitlan. This illustration was made by an Aztec artist in the 1500s. It shows the city's founders seated around the eagle. Today, a similar eagle design is used on Mexico's national flag.

# Tenochtitlan – city on a lake

## Farming the land

*I wanted to know how the Aztecs succeeded as farmers if their overcrowded island had so little land. Professor Paz took me to a suburb of Mexico City and showed me what looked like a market garden. He explained how the swamps which surrounded Tenochtitlan had been reclaimed by the Aztecs and turned into fertile strips called 'chinampas' or floating gardens, some of which are still in use today. The boggy land was divided up and each strip was separated from its neighbour by a canal. Plants and fertile mud from the lake were heaped on to the strips, the sides of which were supported by posts. More layers were added until the strip was above the water level. Fast-growing willow trees, whose roots anchored the new land to the lake-bed, were planted at the corners. Fertilized with human waste collected from homes within the city, and with a plentiful supply of water, up to seven crops a year could be grown and harvested.*

*Farming tools were very simple. A digging stick was used to dig trenches for seeds and plants.*

I peered closely at the outline of the building in Professor Paz's excavation. Its grey stone base looked as solid today as it must have done when its Aztec builders put it there. "If the Spaniards hadn't pulled Tenochtitlan apart stone by stone, the city might look the same now as it had 500 years ago," said the Professor. "Its buildings were strong enough to survive earthquakes – unlike some modern buildings in Mexico City which have collapsed during recent earth tremors."

I remembered seeing a model of Tenochtitlan in the museum, and with that in mind I imagined Professor Paz's building rising up from its ruined base and towering high above me. What would I have seen had I been here 500 years ago?

The island on which the city stood was connected to the mainland by causeways (raised paths) made of volcanic rock, earth and stone. Canals were the main routes in the city, just as they are today in the Italian city of Venice. Thousands of canoes transported people, animals and other goods along the city's watery roads. The Aztecs had no wheeled transport and to have an efficient water transport system was very important.

At the centre of the city was a massive walled square, its boggy surface made hard with rocks and earth. Here were temples to the gods. Outside the square was the palace of the ruler, from where the Aztec empire was governed. It was a large building with many rooms, gardens, courtyards and even a bird-house and a zoo!

As Tenochtitlan grew into the richest and most powerful city of its time in the whole of the Americas, more and more people were attracted to it. With little firm ground to build on, the Aztecs set about solving the problem of land shortage by creating artificial islands linked by canals. They rammed wooden posts into the shallow water and tipped rocks and earth over them as foundations for new buildings. At its peak the city may have had a population of 250,000 lake-dwellers.

Remains of the Aztecs' 'floating gardens' can still be seen in Mexico City. Trees have been planted along the edge of each plot of land. The trees' roots help to fix the floating land to the lake-bed.

Seen from the mainland, Tenochtitlan presented an amazing sight to visitors. This illustration is set in the year 1519, the year the Aztec capital was first seen by Spaniards. Lake Texcoco surrounded the island on which Tenochtitlan was built. Causeways (raised paths) linked it to the shore and at its heart was a temple complex. At the edges of the island were the 'chinampas' or floating gardens and between them were the canals that acted as the city's network of roads. On seeing the city for the first time, Bernal Díaz, a Spanish soldier, said, "It was all so wonderful...this first glimpse of things never heard of, seen or dreamed before."

# The people – nobles and commoners

The maguey cactus was much used by the Aztecs. Its juice was fermented to make a mildly alcoholic drink called 'pulque'. Its dried leaves were used as fuel and for thatching and its spines became sewing needles. The long fibres from its leaves were woven into coarse, linen-like cloth.

## The Aztec emperors

**Name (dates of reign)**

Acamapichtli (1375–1395)
Huitzilihuitl (1395–1417)
Chimalpopoca (1417–1426)
Itzcoatl (1427–1440)
Moctezuma I (1440–1469)
Axayacatl (1469–1481)
Tizoc (1481–1486)
Ahuitzotl (1486–1502)
Moctezuma II (1502–1520)
Cuitlahuac (1520)
Cuauhtemoc (1520–1525)

As the morning heat increased I noticed a change of pace come over the workers on Professor Paz's excavation. Tools were tidied away and the morning's finds were taken to one of the huts on the site. "Time for siesta," said the Professor, and he led me to the welcome shade of a nearby restaurant. We ate a typical Mexican lunch of soup and beans and quenched our thirst with a fruit drink. As we ate, we talked about the Aztec people.

**Nobles**

The highest ranking noble was the Emperor. On the death of an Emperor the title usually passed to his brother, or if he did not have a brother then to a son or nephew.

Aztec nobles controlled the wealth of the empire. They owned land and governed the lives of the people who worked for them. Nobles lived in grand houses with servants. They paid no tax and could have many wives. Their children were well educated and girls had their marriages arranged with other wealthy families.

**Commoners**

The ordinary people formed the great mass of the Aztec population. They served in the army, worked in the fields, made buildings and objects for everyday and religious use. Commoners belonged to clans called 'calpulli', which means 'group of houses'. A 'calpulli' consisted of about 100 houses and was governed by an elected official.

Slaves were the lowest rank and were owned by their masters. They could be prisoners from tribes captured in battle or criminals serving a punishment for a crime.

A picture from an Aztec codex (book) of a captured enemy leader and his family. As a prisoner he has had a rope placed around his neck, which is held by his Aztec captors. Behind him are his wife and daughter, both shown wearing slave collars.

Fact File

## How did they dress?

*Men wore loin-cloths. For commoners this was a piece of plain fabric wrapped around the waist. For nobles it was decorated with patterns and even edged with fur or precious feathers – signs of the wearer's wealth and status. Cloaks were also worn, held in place by a knot at the shoulder (the Aztecs did not use buttons or pins).*

*Women wore ankle-length skirts tied at the waist with a belt. Plain skirts were worn for everyday use, but for special occasions they put on skirts decorated with colourful designs. Women of the nobility wore long blouses over their skirts.*

*Commoners' clothes were made from fibres of the spiney-leaved maguey cactus. Cotton clothes were expensive because raw cotton had to be brought in from far away. Cotton was worn only by the nobles. The penalty for a commoner found wearing cotton clothes was death by stoning or strangulation.*

An artist's reconstruction which shows how the Aztecs dressed. In the centre is a farmer wearing a simple, undecorated loin-cloth. He has been working in a field, gathering maize. The woman is wearing a long skirt and a simple slip-over blouse, both of which were made from coarse fibres from the maguey cactus. She is grinding the maize into flour. The man to the right is a noble, dressed in fine clothes made of cotton. Note that he is wearing sandals – most ordinary people went around barefoot.

# Families and children

A child's rattle. Inside are beans which rattled when the object was shaken.

The idea of having a long siesta in the middle of the day was something I thought I could get used to! Had the Aztecs enjoyed siestas, I wondered?

As I sat in the restaurant with Professor Paz, our conversation turned to Aztec family life. I recalled seeing one of the Aztec 'chinampas', or gardens (see page 14), still in use here in Mexico City and I asked about the family who had farmed it 500 years ago.

That plot of land, the Professor explained, would have been in great demand by the people of Tenochtitlan. Good land was scarce and it was saved for married couples only. Marriage was important. Boys married at about the age of 20, girls at about 15. Once married they became full members of their 'calpulli' or clan (see page 16), but as long as they stayed unmarried they did not have the full rights of adults. The married couple set up home on one of the 'chinampas'. The man was the house-builder and farmer, and the woman cooked, tended animals and made clothes.

Children were especially important to the Aztecs and were seen as a gift from the gods. If the baby was a girl, her umbilical cord was buried near the hearth of the house. This represented the girl's life attached to the home. A boy's cord was dried and buried on a battlefield, showing that his life would be dedicated to warfare. A day associated with good fortune was chosen as the baby's naming day, after which boys ran to nearby houses calling the baby's name to the people inside.

As children grew up they were expected to learn from their parents. Girls learned how to weave and make clothes while boys

A picture from an Aztec codex (book) showing the birth of a child. To the left is the mother with her baby in its cot. To the right, a midwife washes the baby in a bowl of water placed on a rush mat. Footprints around the mat show the direction the midwife was expected to walk. To the right of the mat are three boys eating beans and maize. When ordered by the midwife they called out the baby's name. Above the mat are objects for a boy (spears and tools) and below are objects for a girl (a broom, a spindle and a work-basket).

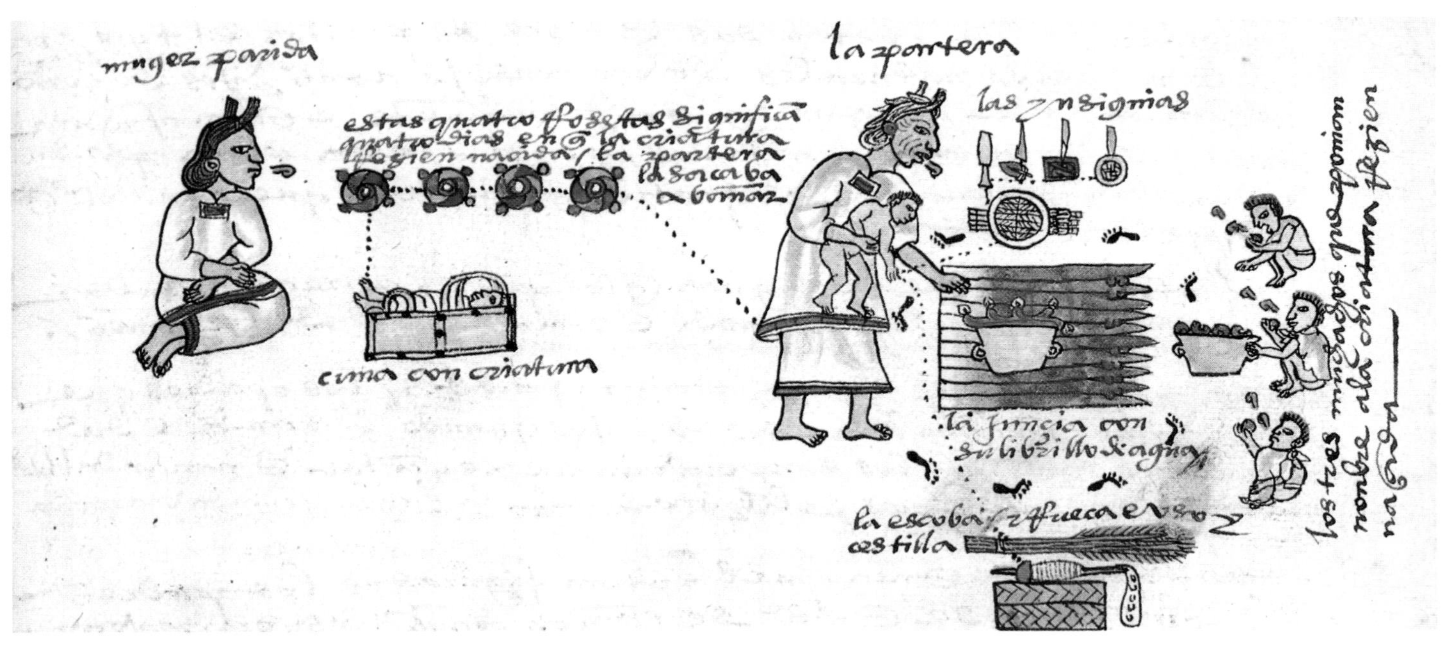

A page from an Aztec codex (book) showing children between the ages of 3 and 6 (1 blue dot = 1 year). At age 3, children receive half a cake of maize per day. At age 6, it was one-and-a-half cakes each. Boys' duties are shown to the left, girls' to the right. At age 4, boys fetch water; girls are shown the spindle. At age 5, boys carry light loads; girls begin to spin. At age 6, boys pick up left-overs at the market; girls spin cactus or cotton fibres. Boys were taught by their fathers and girls by their mothers.

## Fact File

### Going to school

*A school education was an essential part of growing up, where children were turned into miniature adults, ready to face the demands of grown-up life. Children from noble families were sent to different schools from other children. Each 'calpulli', or clan, had a school for children of commoners in its territory. Boys and girls went to separate schools. At a boys' school instructors taught history, religion, good behaviour, music, singing and dancing. Boys were prepared for adult life and learned about fighting and weapons. Their time at school was deliberately harsh, in readiness for 'real life'. Boys from noble families were given a good education as they would one day become people with important duties. They learned subjects such as astrology, government, law, medicine and writing.*

*Girls could have the same education as boys, if their parents wished. But they were usually sent to temples and trained to become priestesses. Most left when it was time for them to marry, usually when they were 15 years old.*

were taught how to fish and farm the land. Disobedient children were punished. One form of punishment was to hold the child in the smoke of burning chilli peppers – the effects must have been similar to those from peeling onions! A punishment for boys was to be pricked with cactus spikes. Girls were given extra housework.

Grandparents and other elderly people were treated with respect. They were even allowed to get drunk on 'pulque', an alcoholic cactus juice drink! Drunkenness was usually considered an offence, but the rule was set aside for people over the age of 70.

# ORGANIZING THE PEOPLE

## Moctezuma II – the last great emperor

When I was at school I learned about an Aztec emperor called 'Montezuma'. Now, here in Mexico City I discovered that my schoolbooks had misspelt his name! When the Spaniards first wrote about their encounters with the Aztecs they mistakenly referred to this leader as 'Montezuma' – a mistake that has lasted for centuries. Today, we know his full name was Moctezuma Xocoyotzin (Moctezuma the Younger), but he is usually called Moctezuma II (Moctezuma the Second).

Moctezuma II was the last great Aztec ruler. It was during his reign that Spaniards discovered the Aztecs and within a few years the Aztec empire collapsed. Moctezuma II was born into the Aztec royal family in 1467. He was sent to a school for the nobility where he trained as a warrior and a priest. In 1502 he was chosen to be the next Aztec ruler after the death of the old Emperor, his uncle, Ahuitzotl (see table on page 16). He was 34 years old and was chosen because he was a strong military commander.

During the eighteen years of his reign, Moctezuma II ruled the Aztec Empire with total authority – no one challenged him or accused him of being weak. He led military expeditions to win new land, stopped rebellions within the empire and governed his people with strict laws and heavy taxes. Despite this he became extremely popular with the people and they regarded him as being sent by the gods.

This elaborate headdress is said to have belonged to Moctezuma II. It may have formed part of a hoard of treasure sent to Spain by Hernán Cortés, the military leader who overthrew the Aztec empire (see page 42). The headdress is made of green feathers from the quetzal bird, blue feathers from the cotinga bird, and gold discs. Feathers such as these were highly prized and were collected from over a very large area of forest. Feathers from over 250 birds were used.

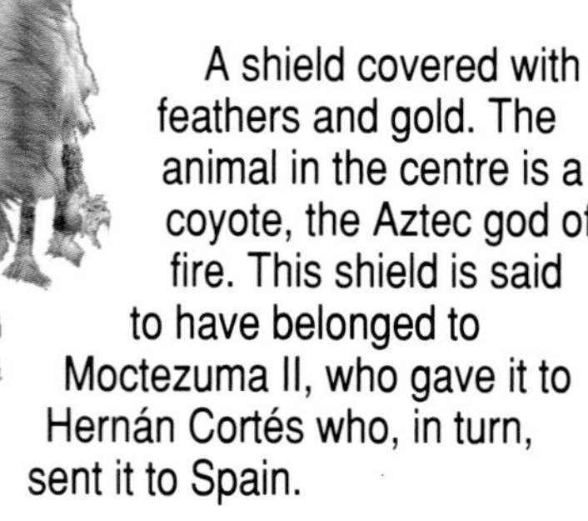

A shield covered with feathers and gold. The animal in the centre is a coyote, the Aztec god of fire. This shield is said to have belonged to Moctezuma II, who gave it to Hernán Cortés who, in turn, sent it to Spain.

Bernal Díaz, a Spanish soldier, described Moctezuma II in these words, "He was about 40 years old, of good height, well proportioned, spare and slight, and not very dark... He did not wear his hair long but just over his ears, and he had a short black beard, well shaped and thin. His face was rather long and cheerful, he had fine eyes, and in his appearance and manner could express geniality or, when necessary, a serious composure."

After Moctezuma II's death in 1520, the Aztec empire broke up and its land and riches were claimed by Spain (see page 42).

## Moctezuma II's lifestyle

*Aztec emperors lived in luxury and from what we know of Moctezuma II he was treated as if he was a god. His great palace at Tenochtitlan was described by Hernán Cortés (the leader of the invading Spanish army) as, "So marvellous that in Spain there is nothing to compare with it". The palace was richly decorated with colourful designs. It was built on two levels with rooms for 3,000 officials, nobles and servants who saw to Moctezuma II's every need. He kept exotic animals and birds and in his garden were plants from all over his empire.*

*Bernal Díaz described one of his meals, "His servants prepared him more than 30 dishes which they put over small earthenware ovens to prevent them from getting cold. They cooked more than 300 plates of food of turkey, duck and venison which was served on fine pottery dishes. Sometimes they brought him in cups of pure gold a drink made from the cocoa plant, all frothed up, of which he would drink a little". What do you think the drink was?* *(See page 26.)*

A portrait of Moctezuma II dressed in the clothes of an Aztec emperor. The portrait was painted by a Spanish artist who may never have actually seen the emperor. How does it compare with the eye-witness description made by Bernal Díaz, mentioned on this page?

# Law and order

Professor Paz and I agreed that although digging up fragments of long-lost Aztec buildings was fascinating, unfortunately those silent old stones could not really tell us about life in the Aztec world. There would always be some things which never left any buried traces, such as how law and order were enforced. In this case archaeologists and historians use written records made by the Aztecs themselves and by their Spanish observers.

The Professor's description of the Aztec civilization made me realize that every aspect of life was governed by the law. I should have expected this. For the Aztecs to be strong and successful they needed laws for people to follow – that way they could be sure of spotting trouble-makers and dealing with them.

A person accused of a crime was taken before a court where a group of judges decided whether he was guilty or not. The judges were specially chosen and were respected members of the community. In some cases the Emperor was in court to pronounce sentence. Court scribes recorded the case details and verdict.

The Aztecs believed in fair trials, but as the table to the right shows, they had harsh punishments for those found guilty.

## Breaking the law

| **Crime** | **Punishment** |
|---|---|
| Adultery | Death |
| Commoner found wearing cotton clothes | Death |
| Cutting down a living tree | Death |
| Drunkenness | First offence: head shaved, house destroyed. Second offence: death |
| Handling stolen property | Sold into slavery |
| Kidnapping | Sold into slavery |
| Moving a field boundary | Death |
| Murder | Death |
| Selling sub-standard goods | Loss of property |
| Theft (major) | Death |
| Theft (minor) | Sold into slavery |
| Treason | Death, loss of property, destruction of land, children sold into slavery |
| Wearing sandals in the Emperor's palace | Death |

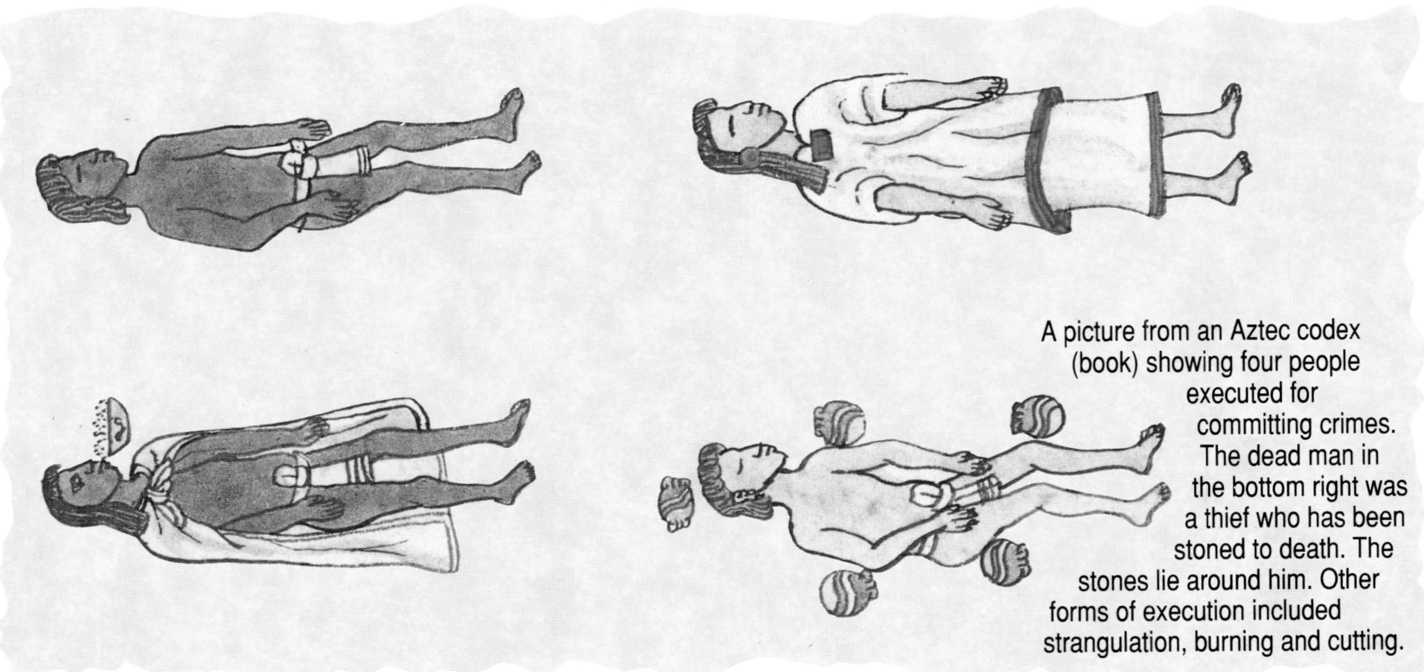

A picture from an Aztec codex (book) showing four people executed for committing crimes. The dead man in the bottom right was a thief who has been stoned to death. The stones lie around him. Other forms of execution included strangulation, burning and cutting.

Fact File

## The Aztec calendar

*Measuring time was a vital part of Aztec life. Two types of calendar were used. One measured 'real' time and the other was used to fix religious festivals. This double system was used to fix the best time for planting crops (based on the real time calendar) and when to consult the gods (based on the religious calendar). In the real time calendar one year had 365 days divided into 18 months. Each month had 20 days. At the end of the year were 5 extra days which were bad-luck days when disasters were most likely to happen. In the religious calendar one year had 260 days divided into 13 months of 20 days each. The two calendars ran together and the same day in each fell at the same time once every 52 years. Because of this, Aztec time was divided into 52-year cycles – just like our own time is divided into 100-year cycles or centuries. Every day in the Aztec calendar belonged to a god. Days could be good or bad, depending on which god the day belonged to. The calendar was used to decide when to do certain duties. A child born on a bad day was given its name on a good day, to rule out harmful effects of the bad day.*

The gigantic Stone of the Sun is 1.2 metres thick, 3.65 metres across and weighs 24 tonnes. It would have taken great skill and effort to carve and it was probably one of the most important objects in the capital, Tenochtitlan. The face at the centre is that of the Sun God, Tonatiuh. He is surrounded by signs from the Aztec calendar which tell the history of the world. The Aztecs believed their world could be divided into five ages. At the time of the Spanish conquest the Aztecs thought they were living in the fifth and final age – the previous four ages had been destroyed by rains, fires, hurricanes and jaguars. The fifth age was to be destroyed by earthquakes.

jaguars

doomsday, the end of the final age

hurricanes

fires

rains

20 signs in a circle, each one representing a different day of the religious month

Tonatiuh, the Sun God

## Weapons and armour

*The Aztecs and their enemies fought at close range with spears, slings, bows and arrows. Obsidian, a glassy volcanic stone, was chipped into razor-sharp blades and mounted into the weapons. The sharpness of obsidian was recognized by the Spaniards when they fought Aztec warriors in the early 1500s. A freshly made obsidian blade was said to be sharper than a Spanish sword made of steel. However, obsidian soon lost its edge and was prone to breaking. Aztec warriors carried wooden shields and wore close-fitting breastplates made of thick cotton pads. These could withstand cuts from stone-edged weapons. Some Spanish soldiers wore the lightweight Aztec breastplates in preference to their own metal armour which was heavy and hot to wear and which was better suited for fighting in Europe.*

# Warriors and warfare

Warfare for the Aztecs was a vital part of everyday life. I recalled that on my visit to the National Museum of Anthropology, in Mexico City, I had seen examples of Aztec weapons and read blood-thirsty accounts of their battles. The impression I was left with was a world of violence, where the Aztecs fought and ruled their enemies by force. But was this true? How violent was the Aztec world?

I put my questions to Professor Paz who explained that in Aztec society all able-bodied men were trained to be warriors. Boys learned about fighting and weapons at school, in readiness for adult life (see page 19). It was considered a duty and an honour to fight in battle. The Aztecs established themselves as the fiercest of all the tribes in the Valley of Mexico. It was their courage and strength that helped them build their empire and defeat attacks from neighbouring tribes.

When war was declared it was greeted with joy because it was seen as a time for warriors to show their skills in battle. Aztec soldiers dressed in costumes suited to their status in life. Leaders dressed in costumes designed to put panic into the enemy, such as the 'jaguar warriors' who wore ocelot skins (an ocelot is a wild cat similar to a leopard) and the 'eagle warriors' who wore helmets shaped like the beak of a bird of prey.

The sides of the massive Tizoc Stone are decorated with scenes of victorious Aztec warriors. They are shown holding the gods of defeated enemies by the hair. The stone was carved during the reign of the Emperor Tizoc (1481–86). Note the warrior's feather headdress, circular ear-plugs, shield and club tipped with razor-sharp obsidian blades.

Four captains in the Aztec army in full battle-dress. Note their shields, spears (tipped with obsidian blades) and army banners decorated with feathers. The soldier second from the left is a jaguar warrior who wears a body-suit made to resemble a ferocious jaguar.

Ordinary troops wore costumes decorated with patterns to which were attached war emblems made from feathers and leather.

I imagined how colourful an Aztec army must have looked – so different from armies of our own age where camouflage is important. In contrast the Aztecs wanted their soldiers to be seen by the enemy, not hidden from it. Maybe they hoped the sight of a large, noisy army would make the other side surrender.

A site was chosen for the battle and the armies met. Insults were called out accompanied by the sound of drums, conch-shell trumpets, whistles and war-cries. Then the fighting began. The battle was usually brief and ended with the surrender of the weaker side and the taking of prisoners. Casualties were light since the plan was to disable an opponent by striking at his legs so that he could easily be taken prisoner. The enemy town was then looted and its people were captured. Prisoners were the real war trophies, since they were used as sacrifices in religious ceremonies (see page 40).

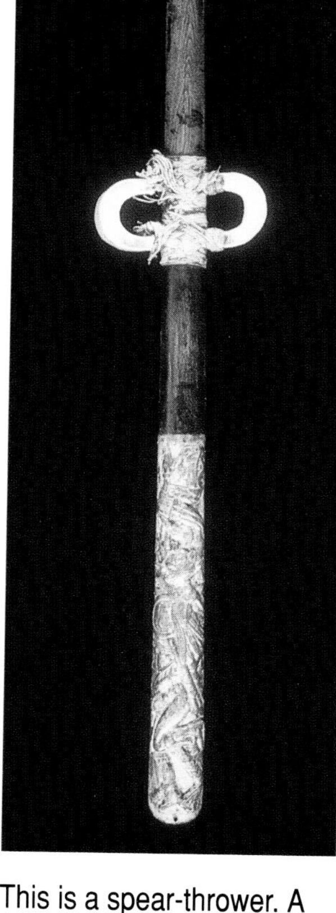

This is a spear-thrower. A soldier held it with his fingers through the two loops. A long spear, with an obsidian tip, was placed along the thrower and slotted into a notch at its end. A spear-thrower extended the length of a soldier's throwing arm and enabled him to hurl spears over great distances.

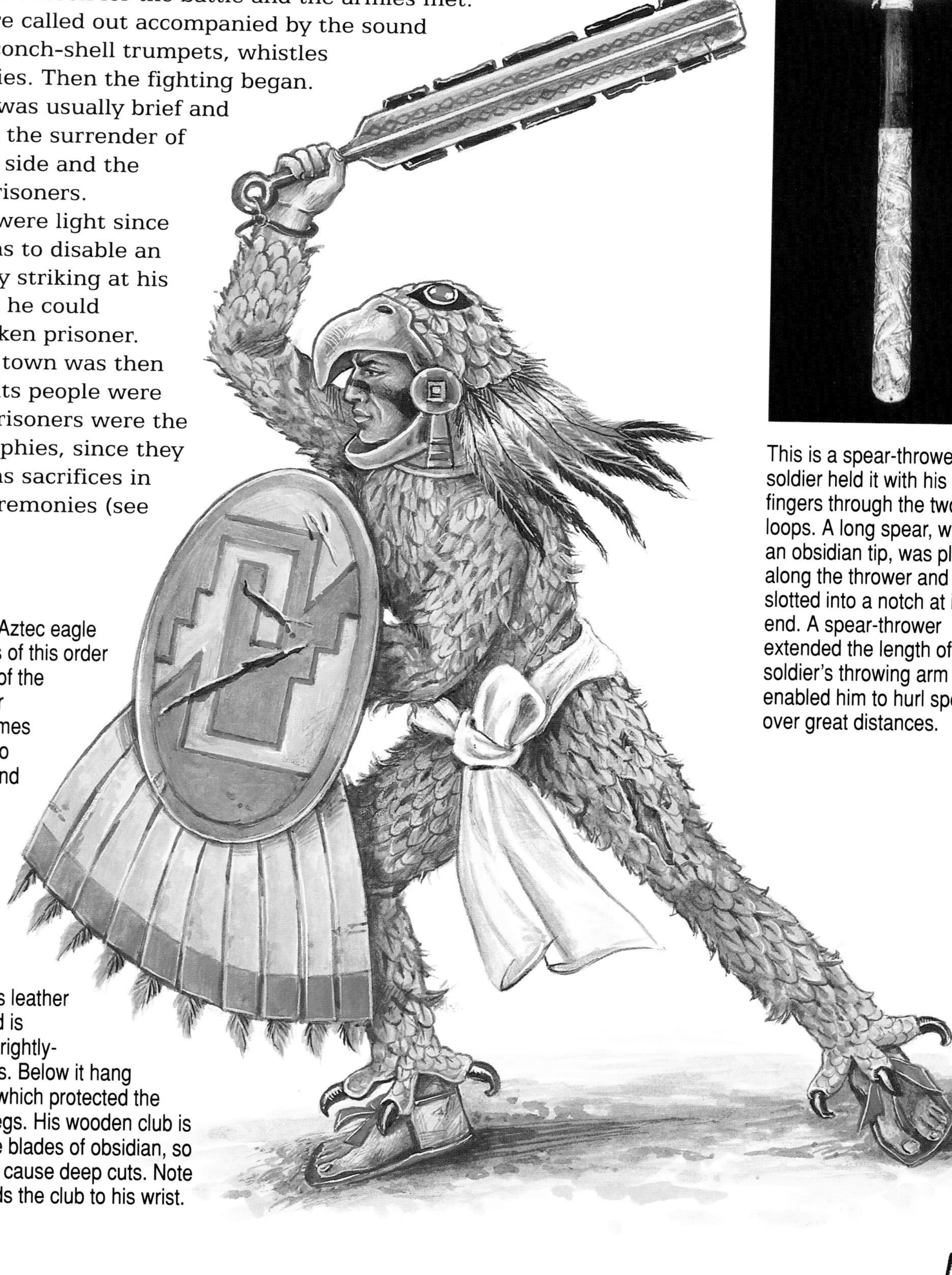

A fully-dressed Aztec eagle warrior. Soldiers of this order were members of the nobility and their elaborate costumes were designed to show strength and the wearer's importance in Aztec society. His body-suit is decorated with feathers and his helmet resembles an eagle's beak. His leather or wooden shield is decorated with brightly-coloured feathers. Below it hang strips of leather which protected the warrior's lower legs. His wooden club is edged with stone blades of obsidian, so sharp they could cause deep cuts. Note how a thong holds the club to his wrist.

# EVERYDAY LIFE OF THE AZTECS

### Food and drink

*What did the Aztecs eat and drink? They ate dogs, turkeys, ducks, birds, insects and fish, but not in great quantities. Their basic diet was vegetarian based on maize, beans, chillis, onions, tomatoes, sweet potatoes, squashes, peanuts and some types of cactus. Bread was made from maize flour, and corn pancakes called 'tlaxcalli' were eaten at most mealtimes. Spices such as coriander and sage added flavour to meals, as did salt, which was an important commodity in the Tenochtitlan region. They ate their food from pottery bowls using their fingers.*

*Water was the normal drink of the poor. Rich Aztecs could afford to drink a brownish, frothy liquid made from powdered cocoa beans sweetened with honey. The liquid was chocolate – a discovery which the Spaniards took back to Europe. Chocolate was an expensive drink because cocoa beans were also used as a form of money. An alcoholic drink called 'pulque' was made from the maguey cactus. Cakes were made in the shapes of the Aztec gods for special religious ceremonies. Most people chewed 'chicle' to keep their teeth clean. This substance is from the sapodilla tree and is the basis of present-day chewing-gum. It was considered bad behaviour to blow bubbles.*

## Markets and food

Professor Paz had to return to his excavation, but before he left he told me that under a clever Aztec law, village farmers had to take their goods to the towns and cities to sell in the markets – that way fresh food would always be available. At the heart of an Aztec town was the main temple and nearby was the market-place.

So, I set off towards Mexico City's Central Park – a shaded area with trees and fountains. At the time of the Aztecs this area was the market-place of Tenochtitlan, and we have an eye-witness account of what it was like, written by Bernal Díaz. This is what he said: "We stood there looking at the great market and the swarm of people buying and selling. The murmur of their voices talking was loud enough to be heard more than three miles away. Some of our soldiers who had been in Constantinople, in Rome, and all over Italy, said that they had never seen a market so well laid out, so large, so orderly, and so full of people."

Imagine the amazement of the Spaniards when they encountered this great market. As many as 25,000 people might have walked along its rows of goods every day: buying, arguing over a price, stopping to talk, catching up on some news. The market-place was the social and economic centre of the city.

▼ Maize was the staple food of the Aztecs. The best seed from the previous year's crop was planted in April, and harvesting took place in September. Cobs of maize were dried and stored around the home in wicker baskets until they were needed in the kitchen.

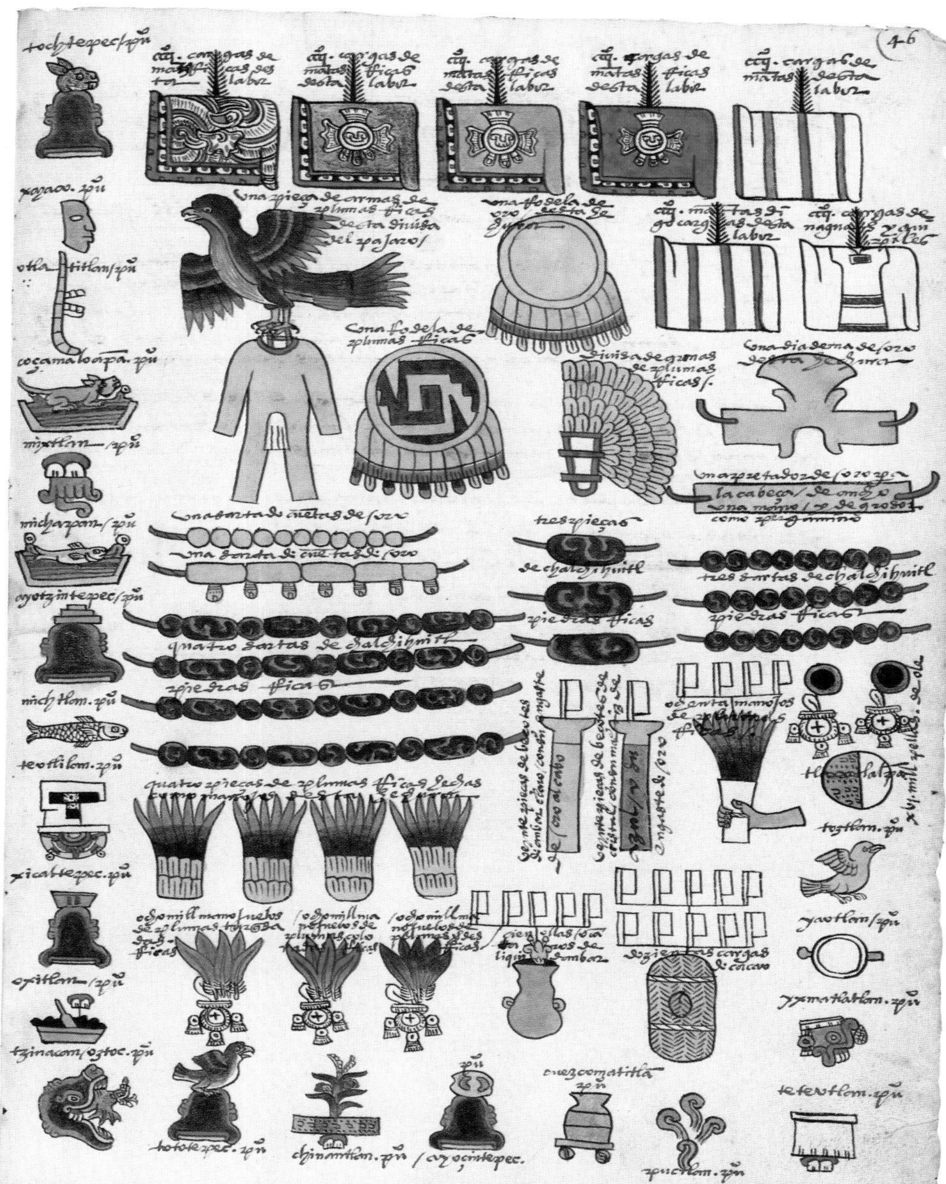

A page from an Aztec codex (book) showing tribute (goods) given to the Aztecs by conquered enemies. At the top are 7 lots of 400 colourful robes (2,800 in total) for the nobles of Tenochtitlan. There is also a gold shield, jade necklaces and beads, bags of cocoa beans, feathers and rubber balls for the game of 'tlachtli' (16,000 of them!).

## Goods available at Tenochtitlan market

| | |
|---|---|
| gold | paper |
| silver | dyes |
| gemstones | stone knives |
| slaves | tools |
| clothes | flowers |
| fruit | feathers |
| vegetables | furs and skins |
| games | edible dogs |
| pottery | birds |
| firewood | textiles |
| spices | glue |

How did the Aztecs pay for their goods? They did not use money so trade relied on bartering, where goods were swapped for other goods of equal value. Differences in value were made up with objects that could be traded again later, such as cocoa beans and bird quills filled with gold dust. Both these items had a standard value and were the closest the Aztecs came to having a currency.

The market was controlled by supervisors who acted like police. They patrolled its avenues, checking that prices were fair and making sure goods were of a high quality. A trader caught selling stolen goods was swiftly punished with the death sentence, carried out in front of the other traders as a lesson to them all.

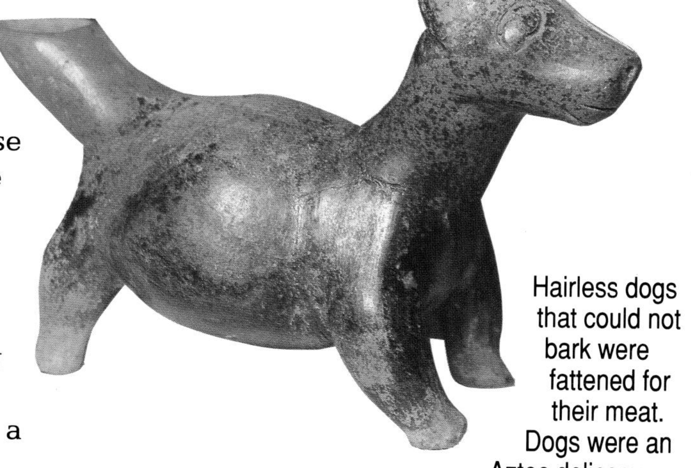

Hairless dogs that could not bark were fattened for their meat. Dogs were an Aztec delicacy.

# Art of the stone-workers

During my stay in Mexico City I saw several large-scale paintings in public places. These paintings had been made within the last 50 years and I was impressed by how these examples of modern art 'spoke' to the millions of people who saw them each year. They told stories about Mexico, from the time of the Aztecs to recent political struggles. Art is a powerful messenger and I decided to find out from Professor Paz about the art of the Aztecs and what it meant to ordinary people then.

We spent a day touring the city's museums and I realized how fortunate we are to have many examples of Aztec art to study. Aztec artists were skilled stone-workers and they created finely carved objects which have survived to the present day. They admired the skill it took to turn a lump of rough stone into a recognizable figure. Stone-workers were trained from an early age and the skills they learned were passed on from worker to worker.

A Spanish missionary, Bernardino de Sahagún, heard about the skills of Aztec stone-workers. An Aztec he spoke to said: "A stone-worker is a polisher, he glues stone mosaic with thick glue, works with abrasive sand, rubs stones with fine cane and makes them shine. The good stone-worker is a creator of works of skill. The bad stone-worker is one who scrapes, roughens, shatters, pulverizes, ruins and damages the stone. He makes a clattering din and is stupid." From this account I could see how highly regarded a good stone-worker was – and how no one liked a bad worker!

What types of stone were used? For small-scale precious objects, green jade, black obsidian and transparent rock-crystal were favourite stones to work with. These stones were rare and were brought to the Aztec capital from many parts of the empire. Jade was highly prized. When the Emperor Moctezuma II sent gifts to the King of Spain he chose jade objects, saying they were worth twice the value of gold. Locally quarried hard-wearing stone was used for large-scale objects, such as figures of gods and animals for temples.

The Maize Goddess Chicomecoatl, carved in a hard-wearing stone. She stood for the protection of ripe maize. Stone figures such as this may have been brightly painted.

A human skull carved from rock-crystal, a hard, transparent stone to which the Aztecs were especially attracted.

A stone mask of the god Xipe Totec, the God of Vegetation and Springtime. Note how his ear-lobes are stretched to hold large ear-plugs.

## Fact File

### To make an object in stone...

*How did the Aztec stone-workers turn their pieces of shapeless stone into the works of beauty I had seen in the museums? The remarkable fact is they worked stone using simple tools of wood, stone and bone – as far as we know they didn't use any metal tools, even though copper and bronze were known to them. The raw stone was clawed from the ground with stone picks and hammers. Once a piece had been chosen for shaping into an object the stone-worker studied it carefully to see where any weak points were. Only then would he start to peck away at its surface with his little hammering tools, slowly chipping the surface to rough-out the basic shape of his object. Then he used a mixture of sand and water to grind the surface smooth. Bird-bones were twisted to drill out openings and cactus fibres worked like saws when pulled across the stone.*

A hard stone called basalt has been carved and polished into the shape of an animal.

# Writing, books and counting

At each museum in Mexico City I'd bought a guidebook. There was so much for me to read and understand. Writing is one of the key inventions of advanced civilizations, and the Aztecs were no exception. They developed a system of writing, but it was quite different from our own.

We have a written language based on combining the 26 letters which make up our alphabet, but the Aztecs used a language based on pictures. There were hundreds of different pictures to represent the Aztec vocabulary. Some were easier to draw than others. Nouns (object words) were easily drawn – they drew a rabbit if they meant a rabbit, a snake for a snake, and so on. But words that joined the nouns into sentences were harder to draw. So, 'the rabbit was frightened by the snake and hopped away' needed many pictures to express the actual meaning of this simple sentence.

Aztec picture-writing was made by skilled people, usually priests or scribes (writers). They were the only people who could read the pictures. The pictures helped them to remember details when they recited stories to an audience. The Aztecs wrote about their history and religious ceremonies. They also wrote poetry.

Scribes sketched out the pictures in black outline first of all, drawing on thin strips of bark or skin (see Fact File, opposite). The pictures were then coloured using bright colours made from vegetables, minerals and even insects and shells. Cochineal insects were crushed to make a red colour and sea mussels made a violet colour. About 35,000 cochineal insects were needed just to make one kilogram of red dye! Oil could be added to the colours to make them even brighter.

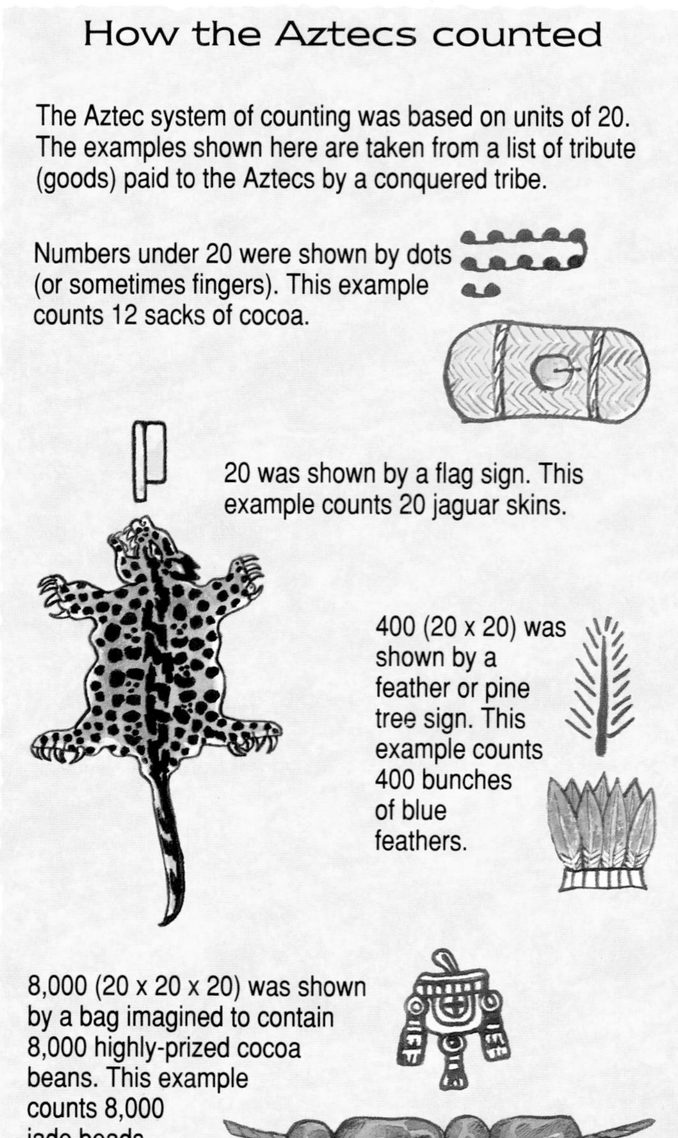

## How the Aztecs counted

The Aztec system of counting was based on units of 20. The examples shown here are taken from a list of tribute (goods) paid to the Aztecs by a conquered tribe.

Numbers under 20 were shown by dots (or sometimes fingers). This example counts 12 sacks of cocoa.

20 was shown by a flag sign. This example counts 20 jaguar skins.

400 (20 x 20) was shown by a feather or pine tree sign. This example counts 400 bunches of blue feathers.

8,000 (20 x 20 x 20) was shown by a bag imagined to contain 8,000 highly-prized cocoa beans. This example counts 8,000 jade beads.

**The Codex Mendoza**
The Codex Mendoza was painted about 1525 on the orders of the first Spanish governor in Mexico, Don Antonio de Mendoza. He intended the codex to be read by his king, Charles V of Spain, but before it could reach him it was captured at sea by the French. Later it was bought by an Englishman and today it is one of the treasures of the Bodleian Library, Oxford. Mendoza wanted to record the history and culture of the Aztecs and this document is a valuable historical record, giving us an insight to a lost world. Without records such as this we would know much less about the Aztecs. The pictures were painted by an Aztec scribe. Near each picture is its meaning, written in Spanish by a Spanish priest. Because this document was made on the orders of Mendoza, it was made in the style of a European book with separate pages that turned. Many of the codex pictures in this book come from the Codex Mendoza.

## Did the Aztecs have books?

*My answer to this question is, 'yes...but different from our own types of books'. An Aztec book was a long strip which folded out in concertina fashion – there were no individual pages as in present-day books. At each end of the strip was a wooden board which acted as a cover for when the book was folded up. The strip of writing material was about 20 centimetres wide and up to 15 metres long – that's half as long again as all the pages in this book laid edge to edge! It was made from deerskin leather or from tree bark. Both sides of the strip were written on and it was read from top to bottom, left to right. There would have been hundreds, probably thousands, of written records made by the Aztecs. Sadly, very few have survived since most were burnt by the Spaniards in the belief that they were symbols of heathen religion. The Latin word 'codex' is used to describe an Aztec book. It means 'from the bark of a tree'. The plural of this word is 'codices'.*

This is the Codex Fejervary Mayer, painted on deerskin and folded in the traditional Aztec concertina style.

A page from a codex made by Mixtec people, neighbours of the Aztecs. The use of bright colours can be clearly seen.

# Crafts of the Aztecs

Even before I set foot in Mexico I felt I knew a little about Aztec crafts. Exhibitions of Aztec objects had toured museums in North America and Europe and I'd been fortunate to visit some. But, on a worrying note, I'd also heard about stolen Aztec objects which were being sold illegally. Once, I examined some objects confiscated from a rogue antiquities dealer – and now he's serving a prison sentence! But here in Mexico were examples of Aztec crafts far superior to any I had ever seen before.

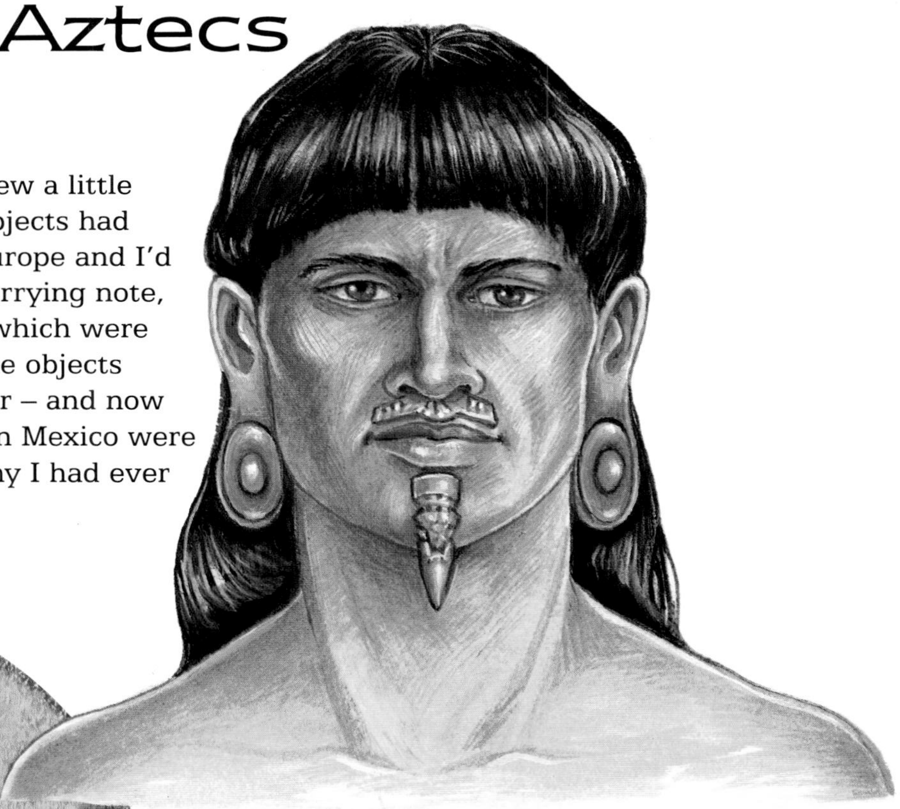

Objects of stone and metal were worn as jewellery. This man is wearing stone ear-plugs in his ear-lobes which have been stretched to take large objects. Through his nose is a gold nose-plug and through his lower lip is a gold lip-plug shaped like an eagle's head.

**Feather objects**

Clothes and other objects made from feathers were luxuries for the nobility. Feathers were collected by hunters who used nets to catch birds in the forests, such as the quetzal with its brilliant green feathers. Some birds with especially pretty plumage were kept in captivity for the sole purpose of providing feathers. Feathers could be coloured with dyes to make them even more beautiful. Weavers would then attach them to clothes, headresses, fans, armbands and ceremonial shields, as shown here.

An Aztec feather-worker using quetzal feathers to make a headdress.

## Jewellery

*Good jewellers were in great demand by the nobility. The most skilful jewellers came from the furthest parts of the Aztec empire to set up workshops in Tenochtitlan, where they made gold, silver and copper jewellery. Unfortunately we have found very little Aztec gold jewellery – most of what was made was melted down by the Spaniards.*

**Mosaic objects**

Tiny stones of blue-green turquoise, black jet and yellow pyrites, together with crushed seashells, were glued in place to form mosaic objects. The two-headed dragon-like creature was probably a badge worn by an emperor or a priest. (The mosaic mask shown on the title page may have been used in religious ceremonies.)

**Pottery**

The potter's wheel was unknown to the Aztecs before the arrival of Spaniards in the 1500s. Before this time clay pots were made by hand, using techniques such as coil- and slab-building. The pots had thin walls and the finest examples were decorated with colourful designs of flowers, fish and other animals.

# Games, music and dancing

When I was growing up I used to play ball games in the local park. I always wanted to become a famous baseball or football player – but I became an archaeologist instead. I hardly thought that in Mexico I would see evidence for an early ball game, and as Professor Paz was quick to tell me, the Aztecs were probably one of the first people to play competitive games.

A favourite Aztec ball game was called 'tlachtli'. It was played in a long-sided court (about 60 x 10 metres) which had high stone walls. The court was shaped like the letter I. There was a stone ring half-way along the court on each wall, about twice the height of a man off the ground. The game was played by men from opposing teams. The idea was to knock a solid rubber ball (about the size of a melon) through one of the rings. Players could not use their hands to hit the ball. Instead, they hit it with their knees, hips, elbows and buttocks. It was a rough game and players wore protective pads on their hips, hands and waist.

## Fact File

### Music and dancing

*Music and dancing were important to the Aztecs. Children between the ages of 12 and 15 were taught to sing, dance and play musical instruments. Some became professional entertainers and their skills were much admired. Music and dancing were part of Aztec religious life. Trumpets made from conch shells sounded long, deep notes, while percussion instruments such as wooden drums, gongs, rattles, rasps and bells created hypnotic rhythms. Bernal Díaz said the big temple drums made a sad sound which could be heard for several kilometres. Wind instruments included simple flutes, Pan pipes and whistles.*

*Dancing could be on a large scale, with hundreds of people taking part. The dances were like plays, acting out scenes about gods and events from the past.*

*The Spanish were uncertain about these aspects of Aztec life. They outlawed both singing and dancing, fearing they were threatening and anti-Christian.*

Pottery flutes played a limited range of musical notes.

This is a small wind instrument made of pottery in the shape of a turtle. It is called an 'ocarina'. It was cupped in both hands and then blown into to produce simple notes.

▲ A stone ring from a ball-court. Points were scored by knocking a solid rubber ball through the ring, which was high up on the wall of the court. Many groups of people played this game in Central America – not just the Aztecs.

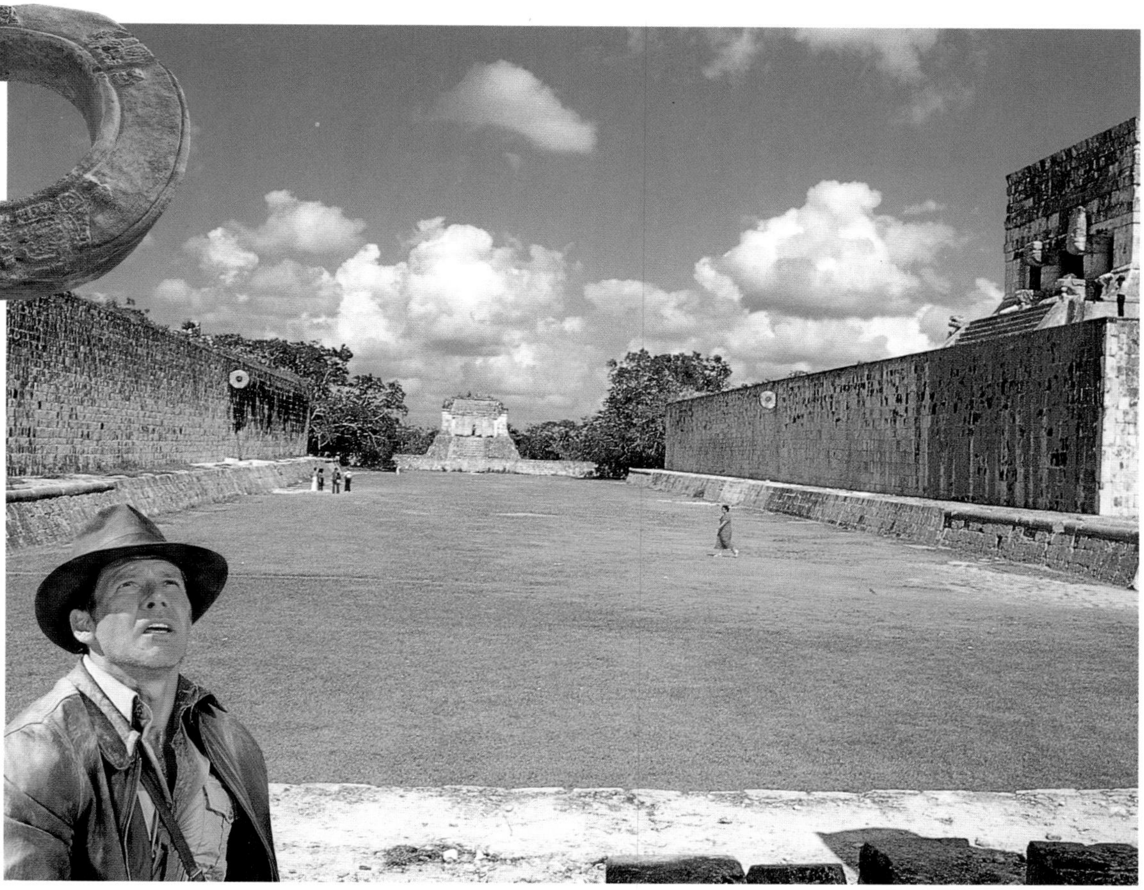

A ball-court for the game of 'tlachtli'. Look for the stone 'goal rings' on the court walls.

A Spanish priest, Diego Durán, wrote about the game. He said: "On seeing the ball come at them, at the moment it was about to touch the floor, the players were so quick in turning their knees or buttocks to the ball they returned it with extraordinary swiftness. With this bouncing back and forth they suffered terrible injuries on their knees and thighs." The game could last a long time before a player scored a winning point. The winner was awarded prizes of feathers and other valuables – including even the clothes of the spectators watching the game!

While 'tlachtli' was a game enjoyed by the nobility, the game of 'patolli' was played by everyone. It was a gambling game played with coloured pebbles on an X-shaped board divided into 52 squares. Beans painted with number dots were the dice. The pebbles were moved around the board according to the throw of the beans.

The game of 'patolli' was played on a board or mat divided into 4 parts, with 'safe' and 'penalty' squares. The Aztecs played this game with beans for counters. It was a gambling game and prayers were offered to Macuilxochitl, the God of Gambling. He is the figure seated to the left of the game.

# RELIGION AND RITUALS

## The Great Temple

At the centre of Mexico City is the cathedral. It was begun in 1525 and since its foundation stones were laid it has grown to dominate the surrounding area. Professor Paz guided me around it, pointing out marble altars, silver railings and statues dressed in shining gold-leaf. And then he led me aside and told me to rub my hands over the stone walls. "Aztec stones from their Great Temple," he whispered. "The Spaniards had no sooner captured the Aztec capital and they pulled down its most important building – the temple at the very heart of their world."

I unfolded my guidebook map. The cathedral was shown and near it was a symbol for an ancient monument. I crossed a busy road to investigate and soon saw the remains of the Great Temple – the most important of all Aztec temples. The Spaniards had torn it down, intent on destroying anything to do with Aztec religion. Its stones were reused to build the cathedral. In time the remains were forgotten and were built over. Then, in 1978, workmen found traces of the lost temple, by chance. Since then, its buried secrets have been carefully unearthed.

The Great Temple looked like many other Aztec temples – a series of stone platforms rising in the shape of a pyramid. The temple was dedicated to two gods – the gods of war and rain (see page 38).

The Metropolitan Cathedral, Mexico City, was built near the site of the Great Temple of the Aztecs. Some of the stones from the temple were used to build the cathedral.

### Temple priests

*A Spaniard wrote that Aztec priests 'went about blackened with soot, wasted and haggard of face. They wore their hair hanging down very long so that it covered them. At night they walked like a procession of phantoms to their temples.' They sound like people to avoid! But, to the Aztecs, priests were men to respect. They were well educated, could talk to the gods and they alone could make sacrifices to them. Aztecs believed their priests could foretell the future. They led a strict religious life of prayer and fasting. They pricked their skin with cactus spines to draw their own blood, prayed at set times of the day and night, burnt incense in the temples, kept the temple fires alight and sounded conch shell trumpets at special times of the day. There were thousands of priests in Tenochtitlan to serve the needs of the gods in the city's temples. Priests did not cut or wash their hair and they were not allowed to marry. The Aztecs believed that spirits would steal their souls if they went out after dark. Only the priests would dare go out at night as the spirits of the dark had no power over them.*

A pottery figure of a priest holding a knife used during sacrifices.

Stone staircases climbed the sides of the building to the highest platform. On this platform, high above the sacred square of Tenochtitlan, were two shrines where human sacrifices and other offerings were made to the gods (see page 40).

From excavations, archaeologists have discovered that the Great Temple was begun in about 1325, the traditional date for the founding of the Aztec capital. It began as a mud and reed hut and was improved and enlarged over the next 200 years – up to the arrival of the Spaniards. Over 7,000 objects have been found buried within its walls. They were offerings to the temple's gods.

It was strange to think that Mexico City's cathedral is a 'recycled Aztec temple' – as one great building was lost, another great building was put up in its place.

The Great Temple stood at the centre of the Aztec capital. This is how it would have looked in 1519, the year that Spaniards first saw it. It had taken nearly 200 years for it to reach this stage of building. Human and animal sacrifices were carried out at the two shrines at the top of the building, some 30 metres from the ground.

# Gods and religion

The Aztecs had hundreds of gods and new ones were constantly added, usually after an enemy tribe had been conquered. The tribe's main god was taken over by the Aztecs and all the objects from its temple were moved to Tenochtitlan where its worship could be carried on. By taking over other peoples' gods, the Aztecs increased the power of their empire. Gods were thought to be connected with the land and sky. Each god represented a different part of the natural world (such as rain) or a part of everyday life (such as maize needed for food).

Statues of the gods were important signs of worship and many were set up in Aztec towns, in front of temple altars, inside houses and in the open air. They served as reminders of the great forces that ruled the universe and the lives of the people.

Aztec religion was outlawed by the Spaniards because it was not Christian. The Spaniards hated the Aztec practice of sacrifice. They found it hard to understand. Unfortunately, we may never know how Aztec religion really worked.

**Huitzilopochtli (The Hummingbird on the Left)**
The God of War and Sun. He was always shown holding a fire-breathing serpent and a shield. A shrine to this god stood on top of the Great Temple at Tenochtitlan.

**Quetzalcoatl (Feathered Serpent)**
The God of Knowledge, the Priesthood and the Wind.

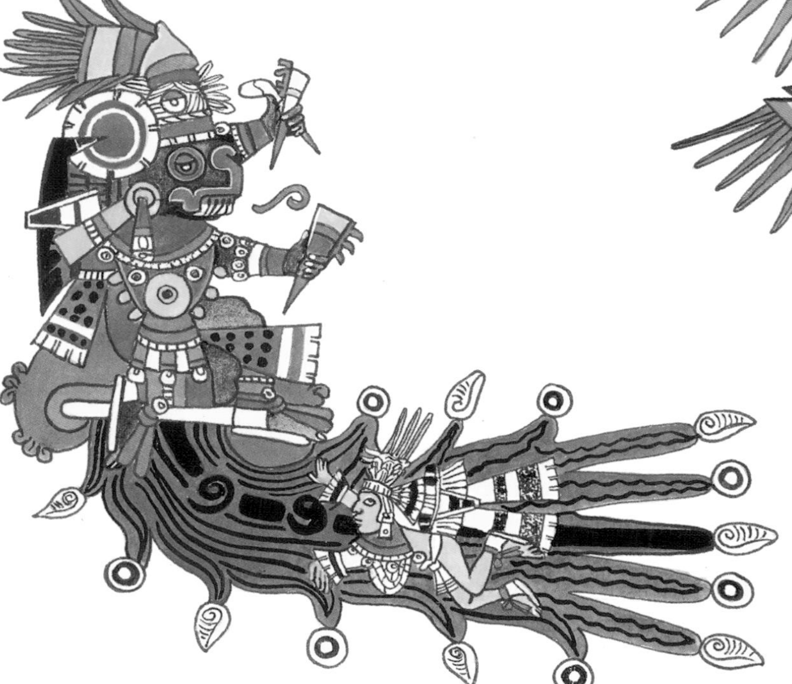

**Tilaloc (Lord of the Sources of all Water)**
The Rain God. He is recognized by his fangs and eye rings and was thought to be half human and half alligator. A shrine to this god stood on top of the Great Temple at Tenochtitlan.

**Mictlantecuhtli (Lord of the Realm of the Dead)**
The God of the Dead. Those who died of natural causes went to live with this god. On the way to him their skin was ripped off by a wind of knives, and they lived then as skeletons.

## Fact File

### The sun and moon story

*The Aztecs told stories about their gods, and one of my favourites is about the birth of the sun and moon.*

*The gods wanted to bring light to the world and they asked for a volunteer to become the sun. Not one, but two gods volunteered – the rich Tecuciztecatl and the poor Nanauatzin. At midnight, after five days of preparing themselves to be sacrificed, they were taken to a terrible fire. Tecuciztecatl was told to throw himself into the flames. Four times he tried but each time the flames drove him back. Then it was Nanauatzin's turn, and he rushed straight in. Tecuciztecatl tried again, and he followed Nanauatzin into the fire. In the morning, Nanauatzin rose and shone brightly in the sky. He was the sun. Then Tecuciztecatl appeared. He was the moon. To send them on their way, Quetzalcoatl, the Wind God, blew hard until they moved through the heavens.*

**Xipe Totec (Our Flayed Lord)**
The God of Vegetation and Springtime. He was worshipped at seed time to ensure the growth of crops.

**Chalchiuhtlicue (Our Lady of the Turquoise skirt)**
The Goddess of Water who was associated with lakes and rivers.

# Sacrifices to the gods

## Fact File

### Cannibalism

*If being sacrificed to the gods wasn't bad enough, there was worse to come for the remains of the poor victim. The Aztecs practised cannibalism. They believed a sacrifice victim had died as a god. By eating his body the living Aztecs could please the gods, too. Only the arms and legs were eaten – the torso was fed to the wild animals in the royal zoo. A Spanish missionary, Bernardino de Sahagún, described how a savoury stew was made from human flesh, chilli peppers and tomatoes. In another grisly recipe the flesh was cooked with maize and salt. The Aztecs ate meals such as these as part of special religious ceremonies. The meals were not meant to satisfy hunger – they were meant to bring ordinary people closer to the gods they believed in.*

As I toured the museums of Mexico City I spoke to other visitors. Many had also come to learn about the Aztecs, and it wasn't long before we were discussing the subject of sacrifice. "A blood-thirsty lot," one man said to me. I asked if his children had been scared. "You must be joking!" he said. "They wanted to know all the gory bits!"

I went away, thinking to myself that his children would have made good Aztecs! Sacrifice was so important to the Aztecs that it was accepted as a normal part of their religion. The Spaniards, on the other hand, were shocked.

Human and animal sacrifices were made to the gods to collect blood. Blood was seen as the liquid that gave life to the world. In particular, it was needed to make sure the sun rose each day and to give it strength. Sacrifices were to please the sun and keep it on course. Birds, usually quails, were sacrificed to the sun every day of the year. People were expected to offer their own blood to the sun. They pricked themselves every day with cactus spines and placed the bloody points on leaves in the temple. No one was left out and even babies had their ears pricked. Priests cut themselves with obsidian blades and pierced their skin with thorns.

An altar on which the Aztecs sacrificed their victims.

An incense burner made of pottery. It was used by priests during religious ceremonies. It is in the shape of a turkey's foot.

Prisoners-of-war and slaves were the unlucky people most often sacrificed – maybe as many as 50,000 in some years. In the most common form of sacrifice the victim was held across a stone by a group of priests. One used a sharp knife to open the living victim's chest and cut out his beating heart. They believed the heart and blood of their victims would keep their gods strong and powerful.

In other sacrifices the victim lost his head or was shot with arrows. Women were sacrificed too, in honour of the Food God. Children were offered to the Rain God. Their tears, it was thought, would guarantee a good rainfall for crops in the fields. In 1980, the bones of 42 children were found buried in a heap inside the Great Temple (see page 36). They were sacrifice victims and had died between the ages of three and seven. When their bones were examined it was found that the children had been in poor health. It seems that only the weak had been sacrificed, leaving the strong and fit to grow into adults.

The victims of sacrifice had their heads mounted on skull racks at the base of Aztec temples. A Spanish witness of these gory trophies calculated that the Great Temple's skull rack could hold over 100,000 heads.

A flint knife with a mosaic handle used to sacrifice a victim to the gods.

A sacrifice scene from an Aztec codex (book). Temple priests hold down the victim while his heart is cut out and offered to the Sun God. Later, the victim's head would have been displayed on a skull rack.

# END OF THE AZTEC WORLD

Hernán Cortés (1485–1547) shown in the fine armour of a Spanish military leader

## The Aztecs are conquered

After 200 years of conquests the Aztecs met people like no others they had seen before. Fair-skinned men with beards, wearing clothes of metal and riding strange animals came to Tenochtitlan. The year was 1519 and the strangers were from Spain.

Hernán Cortés, the leader of the Spaniards, arrived in Mexico in August 1519 in search of treasure. He had an army of 500 soldiers, 50 sailors, 200 Cuban bearers and some African servants. They arrived on board eleven ships and news of their landing was sent to Moctezuma II, the Aztec Emperor (see page 20), some 300 kilometres away. At first, Moctezuma thought they were gods, so he sent expensive gifts to make them feel welcome in his land.

Cortés saw the gifts as a clue to the riches ahead of him in Tenochtitlan. With his army, a young Indian woman called Doña Marina to act as interpreter and a group of friendly Indians, Cortés marched inland from the coast to the Aztec capital. The journey was hard and after 83 days Cortés reached Tenochtitlan. By then, only 350 of his own soldiers were still alive. But his small army was swelled by several thousand Indians who had joined forces with Cortés. These Indians were enemies of the Aztecs.

On 8 November 1519, Cortés met Moctezuma on a causeway that linked Tenochtitlan to the surrounding land. Cortés and his

### The routes taken by Hernán Cortés

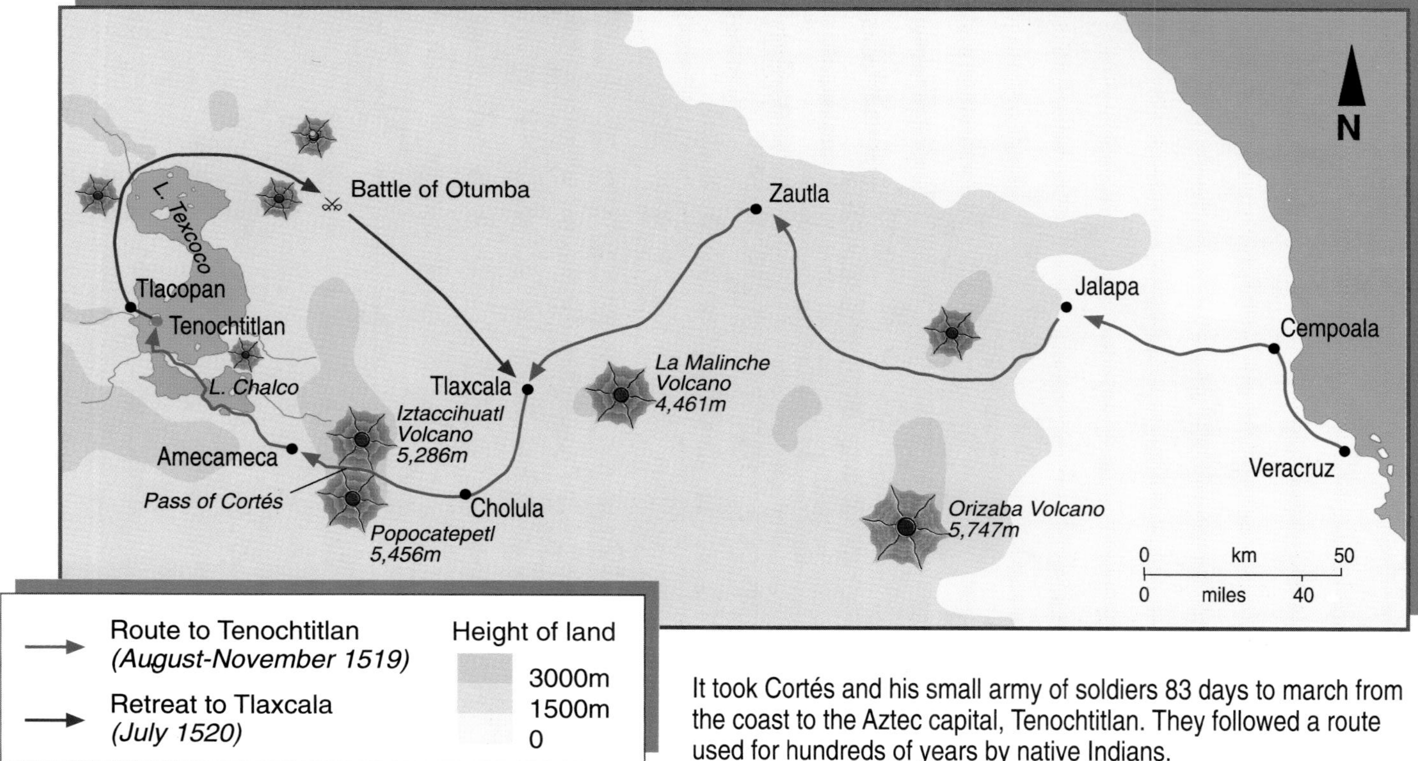


It took Cortés and his small army of soldiers 83 days to march from the coast to the Aztec capital, Tenochtitlan. They followed a route used for hundreds of years by native Indians.

An Aztec look-out sights the arrival of Cortés. This historic moment signalled the beginning of the end of the Aztec empire.

men were allowed to enter the city where they were treated as guests of honour. Soon they began to search for the gold they knew was there, and they took Moctezuma prisoner.

Between May and July 1520 the Aztecs rose up and fought the Spaniards. Many were killed on both sides, including Moctezuma, and the Spaniards fled from Tenochtitlan to Tlaxcala where they were given shelter by Indians who were enemies of the Aztecs. Life returned to normal in the Aztec city – but then smallpox broke out, a disease possibly brought by the Spaniards and which the Aztecs had no natural immunity to. With the Aztecs sick and weak, Cortés returned to Tenochtitlan in 1521. The city was besieged for 75 days and ended with a battle in the market-place. Nearly 250,000 Aztecs died defending their city which was then looted and demolished by the Spaniards. The Aztec empire had fallen and Spanish rule was about to begin.

## Fact File

### Hernán Cortés

*Hernán Cortés was born in 1485 in the Spanish town of Medellín. From an early age he learned the skills needed to be a soldier. In 1492, when Cortés was seven years old, Christopher Columbus reached the coast of America. Soon after, stories of a rich land in the west were told in Europe, particularly in Spain and Portugal. In 1504, when Cortés was 18, he sailed to America, hoping to return home a rich man. He landed in the West Indies where he settled for many years. When travellers showed him treasure from Mexico, Cortés planned to discover how rich that area was and so he set sail to Mexico for his encounter with the Aztecs in 1519 (see opposite). Cortés returned to Spain in 1540, where he died in 1547 aged 62. He wished to be buried in Mexico, but his wish only came true 20 years after his death when his bones were taken there.*

▲ An iron treasure chest. Chests such as this were filled with plundered Aztec valuables and brought back to Europe.

▶ At first, Cortés was welcomed by the people he met. He was treated like a god. Here he is given a valuable jade necklace.

# Discovering the Aztecs

My visit to Mexico City was at an end and it was time to set off back to the airport. Professor Paz helped me load my cases into his four-wheel drive truck. "Feels like you've been doing some shopping, Dr Jones," he said, as he tugged at the heavy cases loaded with guidebooks and souvenirs.

He took me on one last tour of the city, past the site of his excavation, the cathedral and then the remains of the Great Temple. "There is so much still to discover, Dr Jones," explained the Professor. "So much still to learn about the Aztecs. It's people like you and I who will discover more of their lost secrets."

Every year there are archaeological excavations in Mexico City which uncover more evidence of the Aztecs. As modern buildings are demolished the archaeologists move in to look for signs that will tell them whether they should investigate further. A few scraps of pottery or some pieces of stone may turn up in a building site – clues that Aztec remains may not be far away.

A giant stone head made by the Olmecs (see page 8) is displayed for all to see in the heart of Mexico City, reminding passers-by of their links with the past.

Beneath the streets of Mexico City lie the buried remains of Tenochtitlan, the Aztec capital.

## 'Aztecs' today

*Where did the Aztecs go to after their empire had fallen to the Spaniards? The answer is they didn't 'go' anywhere. Slowly they accepted the invaders and as more Spaniards arrived the Aztecs (and the other Indian tribes in Mexico, too) began to change their lifestyles.*

*Missionaries taught Christianity to the Aztecs, saying they must abandon their old gods. The Aztecs learned to speak Spanish and this has become the language of present-day Mexico. The Aztecs and the Spaniards inter-married and their descendants are today's Mexicans. The site of their capital, Tenochtitlan, has become the capital of modern Mexico and one the largest cities in the world.*

Young descendants of the Aztecs

At ancient sites throughout Mexico, archaeologists make records of the country's lost civilizations. Here, a team is making a tracing of the carvings on a stone column.

# GLOSSARY AND PRONUNCIATION GUIDE

**Aztec** – 'The people whose face no one knows.' A group of Indians that lived in central Mexico during the two centuries before the Spanish conquest. They called themselves 'Mexica'.
**Aztlan** – 'The place of the herons.' According to legend, this was the place the aztecs believed they originally came from.
**ball-court** – The playing ground for the ball game tlachtli.
**calpulli** – (kal-po-lee) The family clan to which a group of related Aztecs belonged.
**causeway** – A strip of dry land built over water.
**chacmool** – (chak-mool) A carved figure used to hold offerings from a sacrifice.
**Chalchiuhtlicue** – (chal-chee-uh-tlee-kwe) 'Our Lady of the Turquoise Skirt,' the goddess of water.
**Chichen Itza** – (chee-chen eet-sa) A large city in east Mexico lived in by the Maya people.
**chinampas** – (chee-nam-paz) Plots of farm land built in lake-beds. Often called 'floating gardens'.
**chocolate** – Beans from the cocoa tree were ground up and boiled with water to make a frothy drink of chocolate.
**codex** – A type of picture book which was an official, handwritten record. It was folded like a concertina.
**Cortés, Hernán** (1485–1547) – The leader of the Spanish army that conquered the Aztecs.
**eagle warrior** – A soldier of the nobility who wore a uniform covered with feathers and a helmet in the shape of an eagle's beak.
**Huitzilopochtli** – (weets-eel-oh-poach-tlee) 'The Hummingbird on the Left,' the god of war and the sun. He needed human blood and hearts for nourishment.
**jade** – a blue-green stone valued for precious objects.
**jaguar warrior** – A soldier of the nobility who wore a uniform made from ocelot skins. (An ocelot is a wild cat.)
**Lake Texcoco** – (tesh-ko-ko) The lake in which the Aztecs built their island city.
**maguey cactus** – A spiny leaved cactus for which the Aztecs had many uses.
**Maya** – A civilization of Mexico that flourished between the years 300 bc to ad 1500.
**Mexico City** – The modern capital of Mexico, built on the ruins of the aztec capital city.
**Mictlantecuhtli** – (mic-tlan-tee-koo-tlee) 'Lord of the Realm of the Dead,' the god of the dead.
**Moctezuma II** – (mo-tek-zu-ma) The last great Aztec ruler. Reigned 1502–1520.
**mosaic** – Small pieces of stone, shell, eggshell or pottery that can be joined together to decorate an object or make a picture.
**Nahuatl** – (na-watl) The language of the aztecs. It is still spoken in central Mexico today. Words such as chocolate and tomato came into the english language from Nahuatl.
**obsidian** – A shiny volcanic stone which looks like bottle-glass and was used for tools and weapon points.
**Olmec** – The first great civilization of Mexico. It flourished between the years 1200 to 400 bc.
**patolli** – (pa-to-lee) A gambling game played with pebbles and dried beans.
**pulque** – (pul-keh) An alcoholic drink made from the maguey cactus.
**Quetzalcoatl** – (ket-sal-ko-atl) 'Feathered Serpent,' the god of knowledge, priests and the wind. He was the creator god and was the most important and powerful of the Aztec gods. He was worshipped by other groups as well in Mexico, not just the Aztecs.
**Tenochtitlan** – (teh-noach-tee-tlan) 'Place of the prickly pear cactus fruit,' capital city of the aztecs founded in 1325 and built on an island in Lake Texcoco.
**Teotihuacan** – (te-o-tee-wa-kan) 'Place where the gods were born,' a large and mysterious city in central Mexico that flourished between the years 100 BC to AD 750.
**tlachtli** – (tlach-tlee) A ball-court game played between teams using rubber balls.
**Tlaloc** – (tla-lok) 'Lord of the Sources of All Water,' the god of rain and fertility.
**Toltec** – A civilization of Mexico that flourished between the years 900 to 1150.
**Tula** – The Toltec capital city, plundered by the Aztecs.
**Valley of Mexico** – A large inland basin surrounded by volcanoes. Mexico City is located within this valley.
**Xipe Totec** – (shee-pe- to-tek) 'Our Flayed Lord,' the god of vegetation and springtime. His ceremony included the flaying and wearing of the skin of a sacrificial victim.